Student Activity Guide

Residential Housing & Interiors

M000250204

Clois E. Kicklighter, Ed.D.

Dean Emeritus, School of Technology and
Professor Emeritus of Construction Technology
Indiana State University
Terre Haute, Indiana

Joan C. Kicklighter, CFCS

Author of Instructional Materials in
Family and Consumer Sciences
Naples, Florida

Publisher
The Goodheart-Willcox Company, Inc.
Tinley Park, Illinois

Introduction

This *Student Activity Guide* is designed for use with the *Residential Housing & Interiors* text and will help you master its subject matter. The chapters in this guide correspond to those in the text.

A review section begins each chapter. Various review techniques are used, including multiple choice, matching, completion, short answers, and calculations. After studying a chapter in the text, try to complete as much of the review section as possible without referring to the text. Then, search out answers to the remaining review questions.

Study the examples and material in the text before working on the other activities in this guide. For some activities, you will identify parts of an illustration, match definitions with specific terms, complete a diagram, or make a sketch. For other activities, you will complete a design, perform an analysis, write a report or essay, or collect materials for analysis or a specific application.

To accomplish some of the activities, you will need a 12-inch straightedge, scale, pencil, and ink pen. Several activities will require other materials such as colored paper or pencils, paint color samples, or fabric samples. Drafting equipment, though not necessary, will be helpful for a few activities.

Several blank sheets are provided at the back of this guide for additional activities that your instructor may design. Furniture templates, rectangular grids, and perspective grids are also included.

After studying each chapter in your text and successfully completing this *Student Activity Guide*, you will have a solid understanding of the planning and evaluation of residential structures and interiors. Further expertise can be developed by applying your knowledge and skills to more complex problems and through more in-depth study and practice in the area of residential drawing and design.

Clois E. Kicklighter
Joan C. Kicklighter

Contents

		Activity Guide	Text

1 Fundamentals of Housing . . . . **7** **14**
Check Your Understanding
1-1 Housing Choices
1-2 Personal Needs
1-3 Dwelling Features
1-4 Housing Types

2 Evaluating Floor Plans . . . . **15** **27**
Check Your Understanding
2-1 Basic Areas
2-2 Types Circulation
2-3 Circulation Evaluation Chart
2-4 Room Relationships
2-5 Reading House Plans

3 Planning Living Areas . . . . **25** **42**
Check Your Understanding
3-1 Room Sizes
3-2 Entryway and Foyer
3-3 Arranging Furniture
3-4 Designing a Patio

4 Planning Sleeping Areas . . . . **35** **57**
Check Your Understanding
4-1 Bedroom Furniture Sizes
4-2 Bedroom Arrangements
4-3 Room Clearances
4-4 Bathroom Layout

5 Planning Service and Work Areas . . . . **45** **69**
Check Your Understanding
5-1 Kitchen Evaluation
5-2 Kitchen Planning
5-3 Kitchen Elevations
5-4 Clothes Care Center
5-5 Special-Purpose Room

6 Design . . . . **55** **89**
Check Your Understanding
6-1 Elements of Design
6-2 Principles of Design
6-3 Goals of Design

7 Color . . . . **61** **107**
Check Your Understanding
7-1 Color Wheel
7-2 Color Characteristics
7-3 Neutral Colors
7-4 Color Harmonies

		Activity Guide	Text

8 Wood, Masonry, and Concrete . . . . **69** **126**
Check Your Understanding
8-1   Wood
8-2   Masonry
8-3   Concrete

9 Metals, Glass, Ceramics, and Plastics . . . . **77** **149**
Check Your Understanding
9-1   Metals
9-2   Types of Glass
9-3   Ceramics
9-4   Plastics

10 Textiles . . . . **85** **165**
Check Your Understanding
10-1 Fibers
10-2 Weaves
10-3 Fabrics
10-4 Fabric Dyeing and Printing

11 Furniture Styles . . . . **93** **178**
Check Your Understanding
11-1 Furniture Terms
11-2 Traditional French Furniture
11-3 Traditional English Furniture
11-4 English Furniture
11-5 Traditional American Furniture

12 Furniture Construction and Selection. . . . . **101** **211**
Check Your Understanding
12-1 Woods
12-2 Furniture Wood
12-3 Wood-Joint Identification
12-4 Wood Joints
12-5 Furniture Piece Identification

13 Walls . . . . **111** **232**
Check Your Understanding
13-1 Frame Walls
13-2 Brick Veneer Walls
13-3 Basement Walls
13-4 Exterior Wall Materials
13-5 Interior Walls
13-6 Interior Wall Treatments
13-7 Wall Decoration

14 Floors . . . . **121** **252**
Check Your Understanding
14-1 Wood-Floor Construction
14-2 Concrete-Floor Construction
14-3 Wood Flooring Materials
14-4 Wood-Floor Patterns
14-5 Floor Materials
14-6 Carpet Fibers and Construction
14-7 Resilient Floor Coverings
14-8 Floor-Area Design

		Activity Guide	Text

15 Ceilings and Roofs **133** 274
Check Your Understanding
15-1 Ceiling Types
15-2 Ceiling Treatments
15-3 Roofs
15-4 Roofing Materials

16 Windows and Doors **141** 288
Check Your Understanding
16-1 Window Types
16-2 Window Sizes
16-3 Window Features
16-4 Window Placement
16-5 Interior Window Treatments
16-6 Door Symbols
16-7 Door Applications

17 Stairs and Halls **151** 314
Check Your Understanding
17-1 Stair Designs
17-2 Stair Specifications
17-3 Hall Space

18 Lighting **159** 325
Check Your Understanding
18-1 Light Sources
18-2 Types of Lighting
18-3 Footcandle Needs
18-4 Lighting Fixtures
18-5 Lighting Application

19 Electrical and Plumbing Systems **169** 341
Check Your Understanding
19-1 Electrical Circuits
19-2 Receptacles and Switches
19-3 Electrical Plan
19-4 Plumbing System

**20 Climate Control, Fireplaces,
      and Stoves** **177** 354
Check Your Understanding
20-1 Heating Systems
20-2 Masonry Fireplace

**21 Communication, Security, and
      Home Automation** **183** 369
Check Your Understanding
21-1 Types of System Functions
21-2 Security-System Components
21-3 Home Automation

22 Energy and Water Conservation **189** 382
Check Your Understanding
22-1 Orientation
22-2 Insulation
22-3 Increasing Efficiency

		Activity Guide	**Text**

23 Designing for Health and Safety . . . . **195** **398**
Check Your Understanding
23-1 Fire, Gas, and Mold
23-2 Preventing Property Damage and Injury

24 Exterior Design . . . . **201** **421**
Check Your Understanding
24-1 Architectural Style
24-2 House Styles
24-3 Contemporary Homes

25 Landscaping . . . . **207** **438**
Check Your Understanding
25-1 Ornamental Plants
25-2 Landscape Plan
25-3 Planning a Landscape

26 Remodeling, Renovation, and Preservation . . . . **215** **461**
Check Your Understanding
26-1 Remodeling an Attic
26-2 Planning an Addition

27 Presenting Housing Ideas . . . . **223** **479**
Check Your Understanding
27-1 Presentation Drawings
27-2 Rendering
27-3 Presentation Board
27-4 Architectural Model

28 Computer Applications . . . . **231** **494**
Check Your Understanding
28-1 Computer Programs
28-2 Application-Specific Software

29 Careers in Housing . . . . **237** **514**
Check Your Understanding
29-1 Local Housing Careers
29-2 Exploring Careers

30 Keeping a Job and Advancing a Career . . . . **243** **526**
Check Your Understanding
30-1 Working with Clients
30-2 Model Ethics Code

Additional Materials **249**
Furniture Templates
Rectangular and Perspective Grids

Chapter 1
Fundamentals of Housing

**Check Your
Understanding**

Name _____

Date _____

Short Answer: Provide brief responses to the following questions or statements.

1. How might a house built in Maine differ in design and materials from one built in Arkansas?

_____

_____

_____

_____

_____

_____

_____

_____

2. What type of exterior wall construction is best for a desert home? _____

_____

_____

3. What factors affect different personal tastes in housing?_____

_____

_____

4. Explain how a young couple's lifestyle, with careers that keep them away from home frequently, influences their choice of housing. _____

_____

_____

5. List at least five different neighborhood facilities to consider when selecting a home. _____

_____

_____

_____

_____

(Continued)

Name _____

Date _____

6. The initial cost of the lot and house are a major consideration in choosing a home. Name three other expenses that should be considered when purchasing a home. _____

_____

_____

_____

7. List the three types of space needed in a home. _____

_____

_____

_____

8. Identify the characteristics of cooperatives and condominiums.

A. Cooperatives:

_____

_____

_____

_____

_____

_____

_____

B. Condominiums:

_____

_____

_____

_____

_____

Completion: Complete the following sentences by writing the missing words in the preceding blanks.

_____ 9. One design disadvantage of a _____ house is it may be monotonous and have few unique features.

_____ 10. The type of housing best suited for a unique building site is a _____ house.

_____ 11. Sometimes special equipment is required to install large modules for a _____ house.

(Continued)

Name _____

Date _____

_____   12. Excellent recreational facilities and services are the special advantages offered by some _____ home parks.

_____   13. Home ownership plus the convenience of apartment living are just two advantages of cooperatives and _____.

_____   14. True neighborhood spirit is often impossible in _____ because neighbors move in and out frequently.

_____   15. A home cannot be separated from its _____ in the neighborhood.

_____   16. Homes that are designed as compact, multilevel structures are suited for _____ locations.

_____   17. Activities such as preparing food and doing laundry require _____ space.

_____   18. Generally, the most important step in the home planning/building process is good _____.

_____   19. Packaged home-building materials previously cut to size for a customer's design are called _____.

_____   20. In some areas, licensed contractors must perform certain housing construction tasks because of _____ requirements.

Housing Choices
Activity 1-1

Name _____

Date _____

Briefly explain how each of the following factors affects housing choices.

1. Location: _____

    _____

    _____

    _____

    _____

2. Climate: _____

    _____

    _____

    _____

    _____

3. Availability: _____

    _____

    _____

    _____

    _____

    _____

4. Cost: _____

    _____

    _____

    _____

    _____

5. Taste: _____

    _____

    _____

    _____

6. Lifestyle: _____

    _____

    _____

    _____

    _____

Personal Needs
Activity 1-2

Name _____

Date _____

List the personal needs that can be satisfied by the following housing areas.

Individual space:

_____

_____

_____

_____

_____

_____

_____

_____

_____

Group space:

_____

_____

_____

_____

_____

_____

_____

_____

_____

Support space:

_____

_____

_____

_____

_____

_____

_____

_____

Dwelling Features
Activity 1-3

Name _____

Date _____

Clip a picture of a tract or custom house from an Internet site, newspaper, or magazine and mount it in the space provided. Summarize the key features described in the accompanying story or advertisement. If there is no description, list the features you would want in your home.

Key features:

_____

_____

_____

_____

_____

_____

_____

_____

_____

_____

Housing Types
Activity 1-4

Name _____

Date _____

Read each description below and check the appropriate box to indicate which type of housing it describes. (Each describes only one type of housing.)

Description	Tract Houses	Custom Houses	Manufactured Houses	Mobile Homes	Cooperatives	Condominiums	Rentals
1. Have little or no involvement in the management or maintenance of the living space							
2. Usually are available from the developer in just a few basic plans							
3. Generally consist of modular components or building parts							
4. Defines a type of ownership, not a type of building; buyer purchases stock in the corporation							
5. Are built to meet the needs of a specific household							
6. Are inexpensive, with low money liscense fees, and require little upkeep							
7. Usually cost less than custom houses, but may offer little individuality							
8. Offer a large variety of choice and are readily available, but ownership is not possible							
9. Generally include complete modules of kitchens, baths, roof panels, floor panels, and wall sections							
10. Are unique because they are designed for a particular individual or family							
11. Have a joint interest in all shared property and facilities, such as hallways, laundry areas, parking lots, and sidewalks							
12. May be placed on a permanent or temporary foundation							
13. Usually cost more per square foot than any other type of home							

Types of Circulation
Activity 2-2

Name _____

Date _____

Create a map of the four basic types of circulation patterns—family, work, service, and guest—using a different colored pencil for each. Then color the boxes at the bottom of the page to indicate which color refers to each pattern.

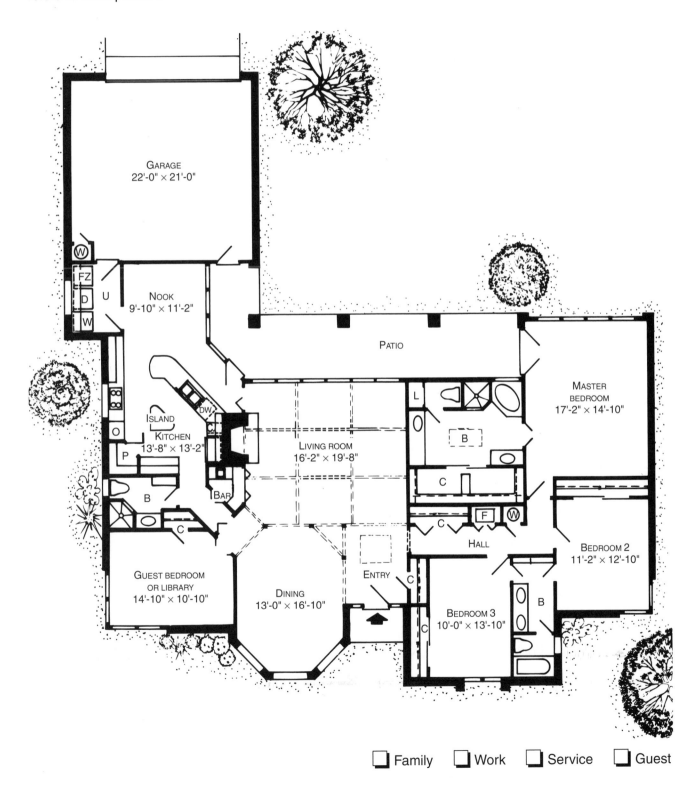

☐ Family   ☐ Work   ☐ Service   ☐ Guest

Circulation Evaluation Chart
Activity 2-3

Name _____

Date _____

Use the floor plan from Activity 2-2 to compare the four basic circulation patterns to the ideal qualities listed below. Then rate each quality of the circulation patterns *good, average,* or *poor* by placing a check in the appropriate column.

Family Circulation	Good	Average	Poor
1. A bathroom is located close to the bedrooms.			
2. The indoor living area is readily accessible to the outdoor living area.			
3. Related rooms are close together.			
4. High frequency circulation routes are short and simple.			
5. Excessive hall space is avoided.			
6. Rooms are not cut in half by circulation routes.			
Work Circulation			
7. The kitchen is the hub of the work circulation pattern.			
8. Circulation moves easily from the sink to the refrigerator to the cooking units and to the eating area.			
9. The kitchen work areas are reasonably close to one another.			
10. The kitchen is adjacent to the eating areas.			
11. The circulation path between the cooking and eating areas is unbroken.			
12. The kitchen is located near the service entrance.			
13. The kitchen is accessible to other parts of the house, such as the basement, storage, or garage.			
14. The clothes care center is conveniently located.			
Service Circulation			
15. Delivery of goods does not pass through a living or work area.			
16. Meter readers do not need to pass through a living or work area.			
17. Groceries can be taken directly to the kitchen without passing through another room.			

Name _____

Date _____

Service Circulation	Good	Average	Poor
18. Kitchen trash can be removed without crossing another room.			
19. The service entrance is located near the kitchen (and basement stairs).			
20. The garage is near the service entrance.			
Guest Circulation			
21. A coat closet is near the main entry.			
22. Circulation from the entry to the living room does not pass through other rooms.			
23. Powder room facilities are near the living room.			

Room Relationships
Activity 2-4

Name _____

Date _____

Study the living room's relationship to other rooms or areas, and list the positive and negative points you see about this relationship.

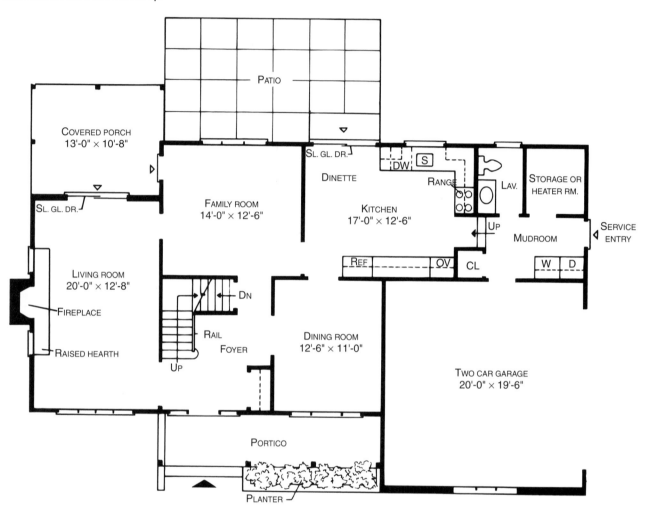

1. Positive relationship to other rooms:_____

   _____

   _____

   _____

   _____

2. Negative relationship to other rooms:_____

   _____

   _____

   _____

   _____

Reading House Plans
Activity 2-5

Name _____

Date _____

Study the floor plan below to determine the basic features it includes and the type of drawing it is. Then, answer the questions below.

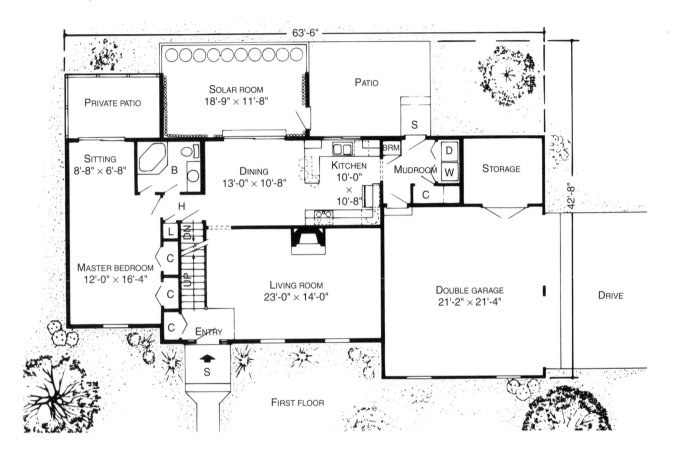

1. What floor plan features are shown? _____

_____

_____

_____

2. Given the type of drawing it is, what features are missing that should be shown? _____

_____

_____

_____

3. Given the type of drawing it is, what features are shown that should not be? _____

_____

_____

_____

Entryway and Foyer
Activity 3-2

Name _____

Date _____

Redesign the entryway and foyer of the dwelling below to accommodate all the following actions: viewing guests as they arrive, greeting guests, removing coats, and storing coats.

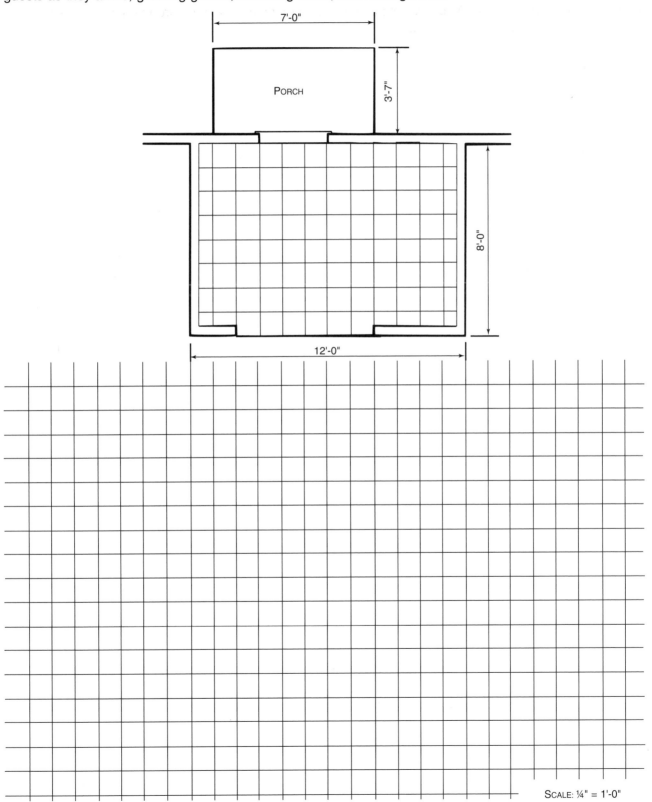

SCALE: ¼" = 1'-0"

Arranging Furniture
Activity 3-3

Name _____

Date _____

Plan a functional room arrangement for each living area below. Use the furniture templates from the following page.

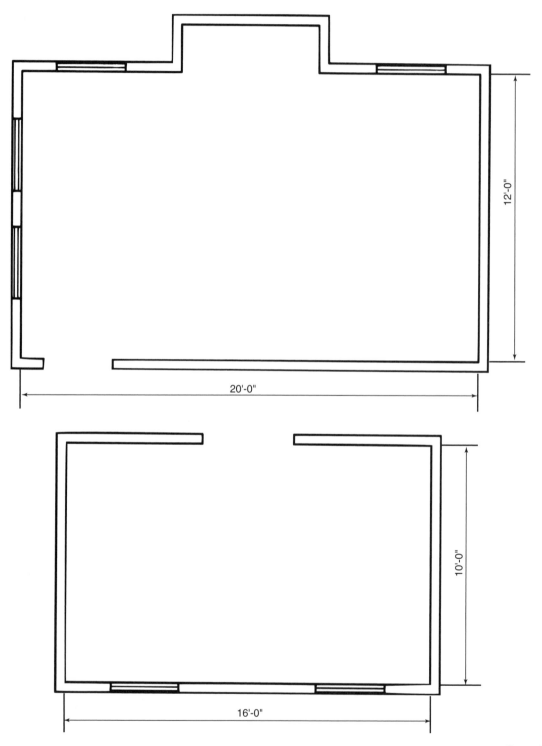

12'-0"

20'-0"

10'-0"

16'-0"

SCALE: ¼" = 1'-0"

Name_____

Date _____

TELEVISION

SOFA

COFFEE TABLE

LAMP TABLE
AND LAMP

CHAIR

CHAIR

- -

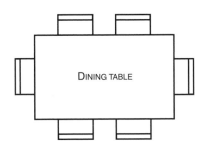

DINING TABLE

BUFFET AND HUTCH

Bedroom Furniture Sizes
Activity 4-1

Name _____

Date _____

Identify standard sizes of the bedroom furniture pieces shown below. Use furniture catalogs to determine the dimensions.

Telephone Table

Length	Width	Height
_____	_____	_____
_____	_____	_____
_____	_____	_____

Night Table

Length	Width	Height
_____	_____	_____
_____	_____	_____
_____	_____	_____
_____	_____	_____

Double Bed

	Length	Width
Double bed	_____	_____
	_____	_____
	_____	_____
Queen-size bed	_____	_____
	_____	_____
King-size bed	_____	_____
	_____	_____
	_____	_____

Desk

Width	Depth	Height
_____	_____	_____
_____	_____	_____
_____	_____	_____
_____	_____	_____

Chest of Drawers

Width	Depth	Height
_____	_____	_____
_____	_____	_____
_____	_____	_____
_____	_____	_____

Single Bed

	Length	Width
Bunk bed	_____	_____
	_____	_____
Dormitory bed	_____	_____
	_____	_____
Twin bed	_____	_____
	_____	_____
	_____	_____
Three-quarter bed	_____	_____
	_____	_____

Dresser

	Width	Depth	Height
Double dresser	_____	_____	_____
	_____	_____	_____
Triple dresser	_____	_____	_____
	_____	_____	_____

Recliner

Width	Depth
_____	_____
_____	_____
_____	_____

Sofa Bed

Length	Width
_____	_____
_____	_____
_____	_____

Wardrobe

Width	Depth	Height
_____	_____	_____
_____	_____	_____
_____	_____	_____

Bedroom Arrangements
Activity 4-2

Name _____

Date _____

Using all the furniture templates on the following page, plan a functional arrangement for the bedrooms below. Be sure to maintain proper clearances.

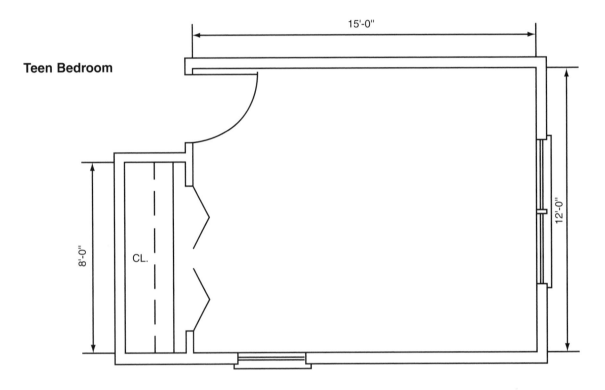

Teen Bedroom

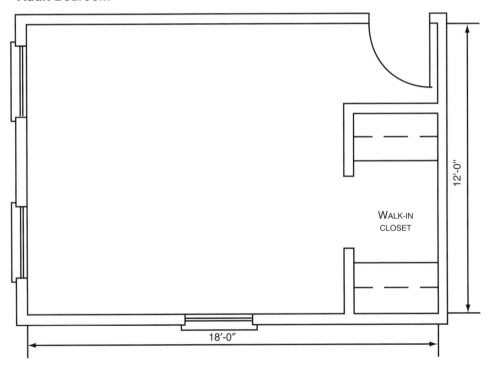

Adult Bedroom

SCALE: ¼" = 1'-0"

Name _____

Date _____

STAND
12" × 12"

BED
54" × 75"

DESK
20" × 44"

CHEST
18" × 30"

DRESSER
18" × 50"

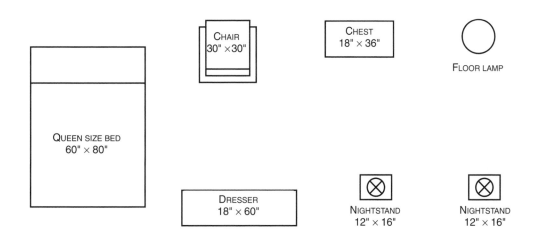

CHAIR
30" ×30"

CHEST
18" × 36"

FLOOR LAMP

QUEEN SIZE BED
60" × 80"

DRESSER
18" × 60"

NIGHTSTAND
12" × 16"

NIGHTSTAND
12" × 16"

Special-Purpose Room
Activity 5-5

Name _____

Date _____

Clip a picture from a magazine of a special purpose room, such as a home office, darkroom, sewing room, arts and crafts studio, ham radio room, music room, or shop. Draw a floor plan of the room to scale below. Identify the unique features of the room and overall size.

SCALE: ¼" = 1'-0"

Chapter 6
Design

Check Your Understanding

Name _____

Date _____

Matching: Match the descriptions of design elements in Column A with the terms in Column B. Place the appropriate letter in each blank.

Column A

_____ 1. Is the ratio of one part to another.

_____ 2. Was discovered by the ancient Greeks.

_____ 3. Conveys height, formality, and strength.

_____ 4. Is the relative size of an object in relation to other objects.

_____ 5. May be formal (symmetrical) or informal (asymmetrical).

_____ 6. Conveys informality and restfulness.

_____ 7. Is the center of attention or interest in a design.

_____ 8. Leads the eye from one place to another in a design.

_____ 9. Conveys action, movement, and excitement.

_____ 10. Rhythm achieved by repeating color, line, form, or texture.

_____ 11. Conveys a softening, graceful effect.

_____ 12. Is rhythm created by a gradual change in the design.

_____ 13. Is rhythm created by lines flowing outward from a central point.

_____ 14. Is a two-dimensional design element.

_____ 15. Is an agreement among the parts.

_____ 16. Is a three-dimensional design element.

_____ 17. Is achieved when all parts of the design appear to belong together.

_____ 18. Is a design principle used to prevent monotony.

_____ 19. Is the primary consideration in determining a design's form.

Column B

A. balance

B. curved lines

C. diagonal lines

D. emphasis

E. form

F. function

G. golden section

H. gradation

I. harmony

J. horizontal lines

K. proportion

L. radiation

M. repetition

N. rhythm

O. scale

P. shape

Q. unity

R. variety

S. vertical lines

(continued)

Name _____

Date _____

Multiple Choice: Select the best response and write the letter in the preceding blank.

_____ 20. A more ordered space results when _____.
   A. unrelated groupings are placed throughout the room
   B. several objects are placed randomly
   C. objects are grouped into a larger unit
   D. wallpaper, curtains, and area rugs with random patterns are used

_____ 21. Examples of diagonal lines used in housing design include _____.
   A. gable roofs
   B. staircases
   C. cathedral ceilings
   D. All of the above.

_____ 22. To achieve proper scale, a logical choice for a bedroom containing 110 sq. ft. and having an 8 ft. ceiling is a _____.
   A. Victorian bed with a 7 ft. headboard
   B. king-size, four-poster bed
   C. double bed and triple dresser
   D. single bed with a 36 in. chest of drawers

_____ 23. The golden section is sometimes used as a basis for achieving good proportion. An example of units based on the golden section is _____.
   A. 1, 2, 3, 5, and 8
   B. 1, 3, 6, 12, and 24
   C. 1, 2, 4, 8, and 16
   D. 1, 2, 5, 8, and 11

_____ 24. Formal balance is achieved by _____.
   A. using various forms and objects to create balance
   B. placing different but equivalent objects on each side of a central point
   C. placing identical objects on both sides of a central point
   D. creating a casual feeling

_____ 25. The petals of a daisy are an example of rhythm by _____.
   A. repetition
   B. gradation
   C. transition
   D. radiation

_____ 26. Functional accessories include _____.
   A. lamps, clocks, and mirrors
   B. crafts, plants, and pictures
   C. sculptures, figurines, and pottery
   D. All of the above.

Short Answer: Provide brief answers to the following questions or statements.

27. List the elements of design. _____

_____

(continued)

Name _____

Date _____

28. Explain how space can be made to appear smaller. Use a large room as an example. _____

_____

_____

_____

_____

29. What are the dimensions of form? _____

_____

30. How can texture affect the color of an object? _____

_____

_____

_____

_____

31. Name the two rules or guidelines that should be used when creating emphasis. _____

_____

_____

_____

32. Recurring squares in a rug design provide an example of what kind of rhythm? _____

_____

33. Briefly explain how carrying exterior design features into the interior can achieve harmony, variety, and unity. _____

_____

_____

_____

34. What is meant by *form follows function*? _____

_____

Elements of Design
Activity 6-1

Name _____

Date _____

Illustrate each of the elements of design indicated below with a sketch. Choose a simple subject related to housing. Use color where appropriate.

1. Vertical lines	2. Horizontal lines	3. Diagonal lines
4. Curved lines	5. Related forms	6. Texture
7. Warm colors	8. Cool colors	9. Neutral colors

Principles of Design
Activity 6-2

Name _____

Date _____

Demonstrate your understanding of the following principles of design by completing the following exercises.

1. Divide each line into proportional lengths as indicated. Be as accurate as possible.

Proportion

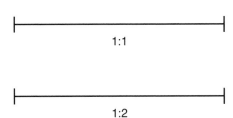

1:1

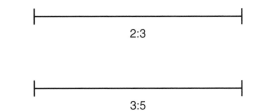

2:3

1:2

3:5

2. Illustrate formal (symmetrical) balance and informal (asymmetrical) balance by drawing common geometric shapes on the line to form a sense of equilibrium.

Balance

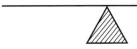

3. Illustrate the principle of emphasis with a sketch or picture in this space.

4. Illustrate the principle of rhythm with a sketch or picture in this space.

Emphasis

Rhythm

Goals of Design
Activity 6-3

Name _____

Date _____

From magazines or other sources, select two pictures related to housing that you believe demonstrate appropriateness and unity, two goals of design. Mount the pictures in the spaces provided and be prepared to explain your selections.

Appropriateness

Unity

Chapter 7
Color

Check Your Understanding

Name _____

Date _____

Matching: Match the descriptions in Column A with the terms in Column B. Place the appropriate letter in each blank.

Column A

_____ 1. Absorbs most of the light.

_____ 2. Use adjacent colors on the color wheel.

_____ 3. Uses three equidistant colors on the color wheel.

_____ 4. Uses a single hue on the color wheel.

_____ 5. Includes the colors ocher, sienna, red oxide, umber, and terra verde.

_____ 6. Uses combinations of black, white, and gray.

_____ 7. Uses two colors directly opposite each other on the color wheel.

_____ 8. Reflects most of the light.

_____ 9. Uses two sets of complimentary colors.

_____ 10. Uses one hue with the two hues that border its complement.

Column B

A. analogous color harmony

B. black objects

C. complementary color harmony

D. double-complementary color harmony

E. earth colors

F. monochromatic color harmony

G. neutral color harmony

H. split-complementary color harmony

I. triadic color harmony

J. white objects

Multiple Choice: Select the best response and write the letter in the preceding blank.

_____ 11. Attributes generally associated with the color red are _____.
A. cheerfulness, friendliness, warmth, prosperity, and wisdom
B. youth, freshness, innocence, and peace
C. boldness, excitement, warmth, and increased heart rate
D. royalty, dignity, and mystery

_____ 12. The color generally associated with coolness, peace, friendliness, hope, and envy is _____.
A. white
B. blue
C. yellow
D. green

_____ 13. The primary colors are _____.
A. orange, green, violet
B. red, yellow, blue
C. yellow-green, blue-green, blue-violet
D. red-violet, red-orange, yellow-orange

(continued)

Name _____

Date _____

_____ 14. A tint of orange is _____.
- A. rust
- B. pink
- C. peach
- D. gold

_____ 15. To lower the intensity of yellow, add _____.
- A. violet
- B. green
- C. blue
- D. black

_____ 16. Warm colors include _____.
- A. yellow, green, and blue
- B. orange, yellow, and green
- C. orange, red, and violet
- D. red, orange, and yellow

_____ 17. Cool colors can be used to _____.
- A. create excitement
- B. make objects appear larger and closer
- C. make a small area appear more spacious
- D. make a room feel warm and cozy

_____ 18. The near neutral-colors are _____.
- A. black and gray
- B. tan and beige
- C. white and brown
- D. gray and beige

_____ 19. The color system that is based on three primary colors (hues) is the _____.
- A. Brewster system
- B. Ostwald system
- C. Munsell system
- D. Prism system

_____ 20. The use of yellow, orange, red, purple, blue, turquoise, sea green, and leaf green hues plus the addition of white and black to the hues describes the _____ system.
- A. Prang
- B. Brewster
- C. Ostwald
- D. Munsell

_____ 21. The color wheel with a total of 100 different colors belongs to the _____ system.
- A. Prang
- B. Brewster
- C. Ostwald
- D. Munsell

_____ 22. The color harmony that uses the fewest hues is _____.
- A. monochromatic
- B. analogous
- C. complementary
- D. triadic

(continued)

Name _____

Date _____

Short Answer: Provide brief answers to the following questions or statements.

23. Explain how red influences human behavior and suggest how it might be used in a design. _____

_____

_____

_____

_____

24. Which color on the color wheel is chosen to create a light, airy feeling? _____

_____

25. How is a secondary color made? _____

_____

26. How is a shade produced? _____

_____

27. What overall effect does artificial light have on colors? _____

_____

Completion: Complete the following sentences by writing the missing words in the preceding blanks.

_____ 28. Accent colors add flair to a color scheme. Often they are drawn from the _____ side of the color wheel.

_____ 29. Bold, warm, and dark colors appear to _____. Consequently, they are used to create a feeling of closeness in a room or to lower ceiling height.

_____ 30. Cool, dull, and light colors seem to _____ and give the appearance of heightened ceilings and wider rooms.

_____ 31. Size magnifies color intensity, so large areas look best when covered with _____ intensity colors.

_____ 32. When contrasting colors are used side by side, differences are emphasized. For example, light colors appear _____ beside dark colors.

_____ 33. Rooms that face north or east receive little sunlight, so reds and oranges make them appear _____.

_____ 34. Rooms that face south or west receive considerable sunlight, so _____ colors are ideal choices.

Color Wheel
Activity 7-1

Name _____

Date _____

Complete the color wheel by using colored pencils or color samples from your local paint or wallpaper store.

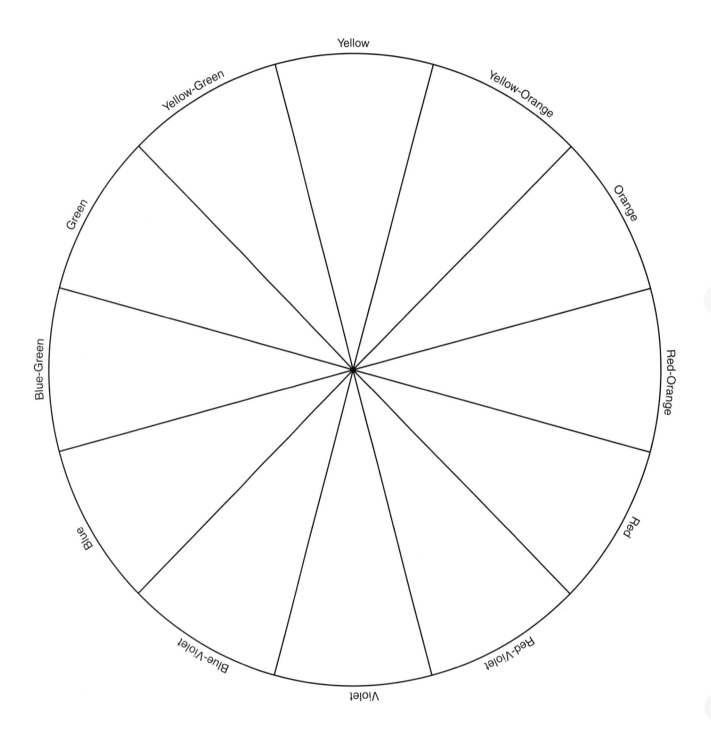

Color Characteristics
Activity 7-2

Name _____

Date _____

Illustrate the hue, value, and intensity of each of the three primary colors. Use colored pencils, colored paper, or samples of paint colors.

	Yellow	Blue	Red
Normal hue			
Lighter value (tint)			
Darker value (shade)			
Lower intensity			

Neutral Colors
Activity 7-3

Name _____

Date _____

Illustrate the neutral and near-neutral colors in the color chart below. Use color samples or colored pencils to fill in each area. Keep the center space white.

Neutral and Near-Neutral Colors

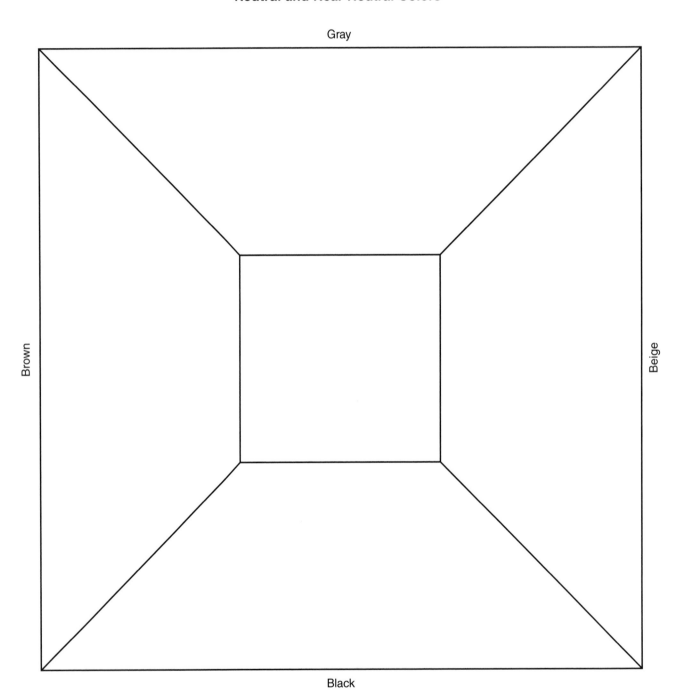

Color Harmonies
Activity 7-4

Name _____

Date _____

Using the color wheel in your text as a model for colors and color location, illustrate each of the standard color harmonies specified below. Use colored pencils, colored paper, or samples of paint colors to fill each required space.

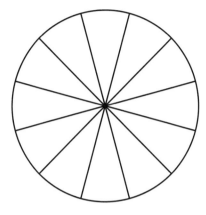

Monochromatic

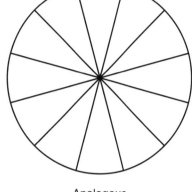

Analogous

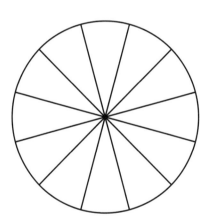

Complementary

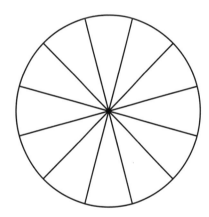

Split-complementary

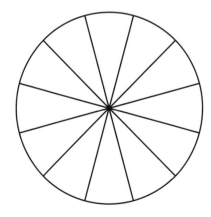

Triad

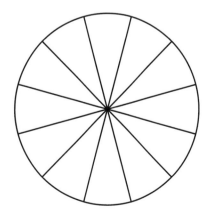

Double-complementary

Chapter 8
Wood, Masonry, and Concrete

Check Your Understanding

Name _____

Date _____

Matching: Match the descriptions of various housing materials in Column A with the terms in Column B. Place the appropriate letter in each blank.

Column A

_____ 1. Lighter, easier to handle, and less expensive to transport.

_____ 2. Used as a structural material where durability and strength are more important than appearance.

_____ 3. Marble chips bonded together with cement.

_____ 4. Building brick and slump brick.

_____ 5. A natural product formed from compressed clay or shale.

_____ 6. A burned clay product that is used on exposed surfaces where appearance is important.

_____ 7. Adhesion of mortar to masonry.

_____ 8. A harder brick that is highly resistant to abrasion and moisture absorption.

_____ 9. Formed from recrystallized limestone.

_____ 10. Pattern formed by the masonry units and mortar joints on the exposed part of construction.

_____ 11. Used for inner linings of fireplaces, brick ovens, and outdoor fireplaces.

_____ 12. Weathers more rapidly in humid climates.

_____ 13. Commonly used for foundation and basement walls.

_____ 14. Composed of quartz grains.

_____ 15. Ceramic glaze finish on the face.

_____ 16. The way bricks are interlocked to provide support and strength.

_____ 17. May have a salt-and-pepper pattern.

Column B

A. building brick
B. concrete block
C. concrete brick
D. faced block
E. facing brick
F. firebrick
G. granite
H. hollow masonry
I. limestone
J. marble
K. mortar bond
L. pattern bond
M. paving brick
N. sandstone
O. slate
P. structural bond
Q. terrazzo

(continued)

Name _____

Date _____

Short Answer: Provide brief responses to the following statements or questions.

18. Compare pigmented oil stains and penetrating oil stains. Indicate how they may be used.

_____

_____

_____

_____

_____

_____

_____

_____

_____

_____

_____

19. Why are clear finishes applied to woods? _____

_____

_____

20. What type of finish is commonly used to provide a soft luster on fine wood furniture? _____

_____

21. What qualities does a polyurethane finish display that makes it a popular choice? _____

_____

_____

22. Name four qualities of concrete masonry units that make them popular housing materials.

_____

_____

_____

_____

23. Assume that you are designing a quality home for a family. List three materials other than wood that could be used for windowsills. _____

_____

_____

_____

(continued)

Name _____

Date _____

24. What are the characteristics of concrete? _____

_____

_____

25. Where is concrete used in housing? _____

_____

_____

Completion: Complete the following sentences by writing the missing words in the preceding blanks.

_____ 26. The two classifications of woods are hardwoods and _____.

_____ 27. The most common types of composite board are hardboard and _____.

_____ 28. A type of composite board made from refined wood fibers is _____.

_____ 29. A process used to remove the natural color of wood or to give it a pale or weathered appearance is _____.

_____ 30. The finish designed specifically for sealing wood is _____.

_____ 31. Carnauba and candelilla are common _____ finishes.

_____ 32. A popular finish used particularly to cover woods that do not have natural beauty is _____.

_____ 33. Structural clay products include brick, _____, and architectural terra cotta.

_____ 34. The material used to bond masonry units together is called _____.

_____ 35. A veneer made from a lightweight concrete is _____ stone.

Multiple Choice: Select the best response and write the letter in the preceding blank.

_____ 36. Wood has many desirable characteristics that include _____.
    A. beauty
    B. strength
    C. durability
    D. All of the above.

_____ 37. Counters for kitchens and bathrooms are often made from _____.
    A. plywood
    B. laminated particleboard
    C. laminated timber
    D. millwork

_____ 38. A finish that evens the surface on open grain woods is _____.
    A. varnish
    B. stain
    C. filler
    D. bleach

(continued)

Name _____

Date _____

_____ 39. Varnishes may be applied to wood to _____.
A. emphasize wood grain
B. deepen wood tones
C. provide a slight luster
D. All of the above.

_____ 40. A finish commonly used on oriental style furniture is _____.
A. oil
B. shellac
C. lacquer
D. wax

_____ 41. The number of bricks 8 in. long needed to form an 8 ft. length of wall is _____.
A. 12
B. 8
C. 9
D. 14

_____ 42. When natural lighting, privacy, and security are important considerations, _____ block is used.
A. concrete
B. glass
C. sound
D. wood

Wood
Activity 8-1

Name _____

Date _____

Match each term below with its description by writing the proper term in each box.

composite board   millwork   softwoods
hardwoods   plywood   timber
laminated timber   seasoned   wood
lumber

1. [   ] Made from thin sheets of wood, called veneers or plies, that are glued together to form a panel.

2. [   ] Product of the sawmill. It is sawed from logs into boards of various sizes.

3. [   ] The hard, fibrous substance that forms the trunk, stems, and branches of trees.

4. [   ] Western red cedar, bald cypress, Douglas fir, white pine, sugar pine, redwood.

5. [   ] Wood that has been processed to remove excess moisture.

6. [   ] Lumber that is 5 in. or larger in width and thickness.

7. [   ] Fabricated from wood particles into panels. Types include hardboard and particleboard.

8. [   ] White ash, American beech, black cherry, Honduras mahogany, hard maple, white oak.

9. [   ] Processed lumber, such as doors, window frames, shutters, trim, panel work, and molding.

10. [   ] Constructed from layers of wood with grains running in the same direction.

Masonry
Activity 8-2

Name _____

Date _____

Illustrate each wall area below with the indicated material used in masonry construction. Masonry units should be drawn to scale with a ⅜ or ½ in. mortar joint. Choose a pattern bond that you like.

1. Brick

2. Concrete block

3. Glass block

4. Stone

SCALE: 1" = 1'-0"

Concrete
Activity 8-3

Name_____

Date _____

Calculate the cost of the concrete required to form the driveway below. Assume the slab is 4 in. thick and the cost of concrete is $75 per cubic yard (27 cu. ft. = 1 cu. yd.). Show your calculations.

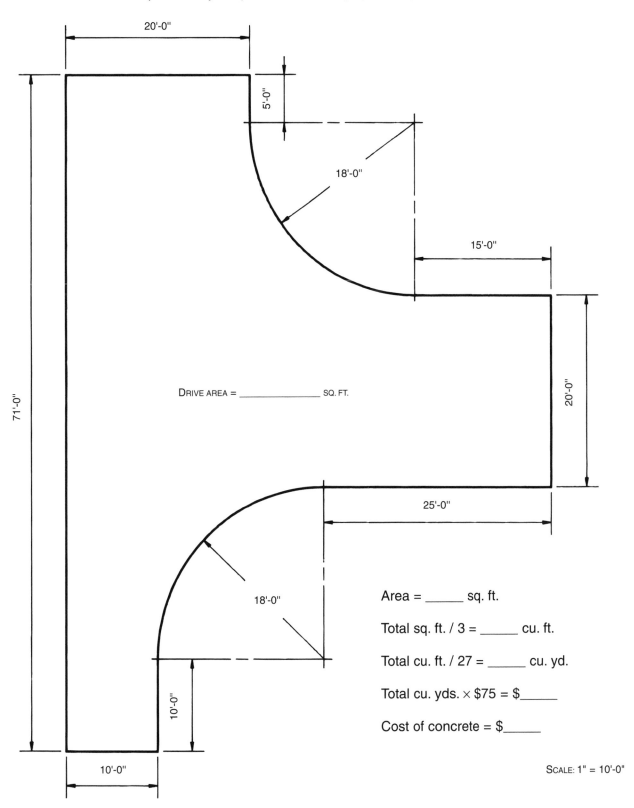

DRIVE AREA = _____ SQ. FT.

Area = _____ sq. ft.

Total sq. ft. / 3 = _____ cu. ft.

Total cu. ft. / 27 = _____ cu. yd.

Total cu. yds. × $75 = $_____

Cost of concrete = $_____

SCALE: 1" = 10'-0"

Chapter 9
Metals, Glass, Ceramics, and Plastics

Check Your Understanding

Name _____

Date _____

Matching: Match the descriptions of various housing materials in Column A with the terms in Column B. Place the appropriate letter in each blank.

Column A

_____ 1. Used for decorative windows, doors, and lampshades.

_____ 2. Used for kitchen and bathroom countertop laminates.

_____ 3. Refers to a metal that can be drawn into wire.

_____ 4. Has a coating that provides a smooth, glossy finish that resists stains.

_____ 5. Refers to the amount of force that an object can withstand.

_____ 6. Is a type of pottery that has a rough, porous finish.

_____ 7. Refers to a metal's ability to be formed into sheets.

_____ 8. Made of porcelain or natural clay.

_____ 9. Is lightweight, highly resistant to corrosion, and a good reflector of heat and light.

_____ 10. Is characteristic of Spanish or Mediterranean architecture.

_____ 11. Contains chromium.

Column B

A. aluminum
B. ceramic mosaic tile
C. ductile
D. earthenware
E. glazed tile
F. leaded glass and stained glass
G. malleable
H. plastics
I. roofing tile
J. stainless steel
K. tensile strength

Short Answer: Provide brief responses to the following questions or statements.

12. List four characteristics of metals that make them useful as housing materials. _____

_____

_____

_____

_____

(continued)

Name _____

Date _____

13. What are the seven metals most commonly used in housing? _____

_____

_____

14. What metals make bronze? What metal increases its hardness? _____

_____

_____

15. What kind of window glass is used in homes built today? _____

_____

_____

16. What two types of window glass are available to reduce heat gain in homes in hot climates?
     Which is more efficient? _____

_____

_____

17. Compare the production and uses of handblown and molded glass. _____

_____

_____

_____

_____

_____

_____

_____

18. How is stoneware primarily used in the home? _____

_____

Multiple Choice: Select the best response and write the letter in the preceding blank.

_____   19. Of the following items, _____ are most likely to be made of wrought iron.
                 A. sewer lines
                 B. gas pipes
                 C. fences
                 D. waste disposal pipe

_____   20. Frequently used housing items are often made of stainless steel because it _____.
                 A. resists corrosion and tarnish
                 B. maintains a bright and shiny appearance
                 C. holds a sharp edge longer than carbon steel
                 D. All of the above.

(continued)

Name _____

Date _____

_____ 21. A thin coating of green carbonate forms when _____ is exposed to air.
   A. stainless steel
   B. copper
   C. wrought iron
   D. cast aluminum

_____ 22. Brass, made primarily of copper and zinc, may also include small amounts of _____ to help prevent corrosion and tarnishing.
   A. tin
   B. aluminum
   C. iron
   D. lead

_____ 23. A type of decorative glass that is produced by applying gem-cutting techniques is _____.
   A. patterned glass
   B. etched glass
   C. cut glass
   D. enameled glass

_____ 24. The type of glass appropriate for use in an oven door is _____.
   A. insulating glass
   B. reflective glass
   C. tinted glass
   D. molded glass

_____ 25. A product that is made from clay or shale and fired at high temperatures is _____.
   A. handblown glass
   B. copper-bearing steel
   C. ceramic tile
   D. cast aluminum

_____ 26. Tiles made from natural clays and shales that are the strongest of the ceramic tiles are _____.
   A. glazed tiles
   B. quarry tiles and pavers
   C. porcelain mosaic tiles
   D. clay mosaic tiles

_____ 27. Fine dinnerware is most likely made from _____, which is a type of pottery.
   A. earthenware
   B. stoneware
   C. porcelain
   D. All of the above.

Metals
Activity 9-1

Name _____

Date _____

Briefly list as many applications as you can of the metals commonly used in housing structures and furnishings.

1. Cast iron: _____

   _____

   _____

2. Wrought iron: _____

   _____

   _____

3. Copper-bearing steel: _____

   _____

   _____

4. Weathering steel: _____

   _____

   _____

5. Stainless steel: _____

   _____

   _____

6. Extruded aluminum: _____

   _____

   _____

7. Cast aluminum: _____

   _____

   _____

8. Rolled aluminum: _____

   _____

   _____

9. Copper: _____

   _____

   _____

10. Brass: _____

   _____

   _____

11. Bronze: _____

   _____

   _____

12. Lead: _____

   _____

   _____

Types of Glass
Activity 9-2

Name _____

Date _____

Match each type of glass below with the description or application that best identifies it. Write the correct term in each box.

cut glass   handblown glass   molded glass   reflective glass
enameled glass   insulating glass   patterned glass   sheet glass
etched glass   leaded or stained glass   plate glass   tinted glass
float glass

1. [   ]   Used in housing structures and some appliances to reduce heat loss or gain.

2. [   ]   Is still sometimes found in very old homes, causing vision distortion due to the rippled quality.

3. [   ]   Used to provide a comfortable interior. Is made by adding a coloring agent to a batch of molten glass.

4. [   ]   Represents about 95 percent of flat glass in the country. Is smooth and polished on both sides.

5. [   ]   Treated with hydrofluoric acid to produce a frosted effect.

6. [   ]   Also called environmental glass, is very effective in reducing heat gain.

7. [   ]   Has cut surfaces that break up light and make the cut edges sparkle.

8. [   ]   Is more expensive to produce than float glass, but has similar quality.

9. [   ]   Is expensive, but desired for its beauty and individual character. Used for art pieces and vases.

10. [   ]   Made by setting small pieces of clear or colored glass into strips of lead or copper foil.

11. [   ]   Has transparent or solid colors applied to its surface.

12. [   ]   Used for partitions in bathrooms or other areas where privacy is desired.

13. [   ]   Is less expensive than handblown items. Made by machine using wood or cast iron molds.

Ceramics
Activity 9-3

Name _____

Date _____

List the typical sizes and applications of ceramic tile in the top table. In the bottom table, identify the firing temperatures of pottery and describe their qualities and applications.

Ceramic Tile

Type	Sizes	Applications
1. Glazed tile		
2. Mosaic tile		
3. Quarry tile		
4. Pavers		

Pottery

Type	Firing Temperature	Qualities/Application
5. Earthenware		
6. Stoneware		
7. Porcelain		

Plastics
Activity 9-4

Name _____

Date _____

Match the descriptions in Column A with the correct plastics listed in Column B. Place the appropriate letter in each blank. Refer, as needed, to the following charts in the text's appendix: A-16, "Thermoplastics," and A-17, "Thermosetting Plastics."

Column A

_____ 1. Thermoplastic used in vapor barriers in walls and floors. Is flexible, tough, and easily colored. Has a waxy feel.

_____ 2. Thermosetting plastic used in molded hardware, electrical fittings, adhesives, and insulating foam.

_____ 3. Thermoplastic used in skylights, translucent panels, and carpeting. Transmits light, resists weather, and accepts colors.

_____ 4. Thermosetting plastic used in paints, enamels, and circuit breakers. Is opaque, tough, and moisture resistant.

_____ 5. Thermoplastic used in pipes and tubing, simulated leather, gutters, siding, and upholstery. Has good strength and toughness.

_____ 6. Thermoplastic used in gaskets, tape, and linings of pots and pans. Is stick-resistant.

_____ 7. Thermosetting plastic used for decorative laminates, countertops, and switch plates. Is hard, durable, and chemical resistant.

_____ 8. Thermosetting plastic used in coatings, sealants, and masonry waterproofing. Is odorless, tasteless, elastic, and nontoxic.

_____ 9. Thermoplastic used in textiles, drawer slides, rollers, and hinges. Is tough, and resists abrasion and chemical attack.

_____ 10. Thermoplastic used in window glazing, lighting globes, and bottles. Is transparent with high-impact strength.

Column B

A. acrylics

B. alkyds

C. melamines

D. polyamides (nylon)

E. polycarbonates

F. polyethylenes

G. silicones

H. tetrafluorethylene

I. ureas

J. vinyls

Fabrics
Activity 10-3

Name _____

Date _____

Collect samples of the fabrics indicated below. Mount the samples in the appropriate spaces.

Weft or warp knit	Felt made directly from wool fibers
Nonwoven fabric made by bonding fibers (other than wool), yarns, or filaments by mechanical or chemical means	Films made from synthetic solutions and formed into thin sheets
Foams made from a rubber or polyurethane substance and air	Leather made from the skin or hide of an animal

Fabric Dyeing and Printing
Activity 10-4

Name _____

Date _____

Give a description of each of the fabric dyeing and printing methods identified below.

1. Piece dyeing: _____

_____

_____

_____

_____

_____

_____

_____

2. Roller printing: _____

_____

_____

_____

_____

_____

_____

_____

_____

3. Rotary screen printing: _____

_____

_____

_____

_____

_____

_____

_____

_____

4. Block printing: _____

_____

_____

_____

_____

_____

_____

Chapter 11
Furniture Styles

Check Your Understanding

Name _____

Date _____

Short Answer: Provide brief responses to the following questions or statements.

1. How does the Regence style of furniture differ from the Baroque? _____

_____

_____

2. What change took place in the style of motifs during the Directoire period of furniture design?

_____

_____

3. How does the William and Mary style of furniture differ from the Jacobean? _____

_____

_____

_____

_____

_____

_____

4. Identify four characteristics of Hepplewhite's furniture. _____

_____

_____

_____

5. What effect did the furniture designs of Europe have on those in America? _____

_____

_____

_____

_____

(continued)

Name _____

Date _____

Multiple Choice: Select the best response and write the letter in the preceding blank.

_____ 6. During the Late Renaissance period in France, furniture styles were _____.
A. large and upright
B. small and slender
C. low and sleek
D. void of decoration

_____ 7. Shells, foliage, shepherd's crooks, and musical instruments were the basis for ornamentation during the _____ period.
A. Late Renaissance
B. Baroque
C. Rococo
D. Regence

_____ 8. The Empire style was influenced by Napoleon's political and military power. This is evident by the appearance of _____ on the furniture designs of that period.
A. Napoleon's family crest
B. Napoleon's initial
C. increased carving
D. Oriental designs

_____ 9. The Jacobean period saw an emphasis on _____.
A. more ornamentation
B. large and heavy designs
C. turning and fluting
D. chair designs

_____ 10. The Queen Anne period in England is known for a greater _____ influence in furniture designs.
A. Oriental
B. Italian
C. Roman
D. Egyptian

_____ 11. Thomas Sheraton incorporated _____ into his furniture designs.
A. subtle curves
B. mechanical devices such as disappearing drawers and secret compartments
C. chair backs in the shape of shields
D. All of the above.

_____ 12. The standard piece of furniture among American colonists was the _____.
A. writing table
B. shield back chair
C. chest
D. rosewood bed

_____ 13. Symbols appearing on furniture during the Federal period included _____.
A. geometric and floral patterns
B. eagles, cornucopias, fruits, flowers, and spiral turnings
C. mushrooms, bells, and inverted cups
D. political and military insignia

(continued)

Name _____

Date _____

_____ 14. American furniture designs were adapted to machines during the _____ period.
   A. Federal
   B. Post Federal
   C. American Georgian
   D. Early American

_____ 15. Creating furniture that was beautiful for its artistic merit and not its cost was the theme of the _____ period.
   A. Art Nouveau
   B. Post Federal
   C. Federal
   D. American Georgian

Completion: Complete the following sentences by writing the missing words in the preceding blanks.

_____ 16. Wooden inlays used to create patterns in furniture finishes are called _____.

_____ 17. An alloy of copper and zinc with a goldlike appearance used for furniture decoration is _____.

_____ 18. The technique of using dazzling inlays of pewter, brass, and semitransparent tortoiseshell on furniture is _____ work.

_____ 19. A carved furniture support in the shape of an animal leg is the _____ leg.

_____ 20. The term used to describe the arts of the Middle Ages is _____.

_____ 21. A scrolled leaf pattern, generally symmetrical in design, is called _____.

_____ 22. A melon-shaped carving used to decorate furniture supports of Elizabethan furniture is the _____ form.

_____ 23. A chair typical of the Elizabethan period with a rectangular wooden seat, turned or column legs, and a carved or inlaid wooden back is a _____ chair.

_____ 24. Caricatures of human heads used for decoration on furniture are called _____ work.

_____ 25. Short, turned pieces of wood divided in half that are used to decorate furniture are called _____ _____.

_____ 26. A relatively inexpensive technique of finishing woods with an appearance similar to Oriental lacquer is _____.

_____ 27. A chair whose back has a pattern of interlaced ribbons is the _____ chair.

_____ 28. Chairs with vertical posts running across the back are called _____ chairs.

_____ 29. A series of homes called _____ style were designed and built by Frank Lloyd Wright.

_____ 30. Furniture of the twenty-first century includes Contemporary, Traditional, Casual, Country, and _____ styles.

_____ 31. _____ furniture is made by weaving various natural or synthetic materials such as willow, reed, rattan, or spirally twisted paper around a frame.

_____ 32. _____ furniture is an outgrowth of the lifestyles and needs of rural folk.

Furniture Terms
Activity 11-1

Name _____

Date _____

Match each description in Column A with the correct furniture term in Column B. Place the appropriate letter in each blank.

Column A

_____ 1. A furniture support that has the shape of a flattened ball.

_____ 2. A very plain table consisting of a wood frame as a support and a wood slab on top.

_____ 3. A furniture foot featuring a scroll design in an *S* or *C* shape.

_____ 4. In ancient Greek and Roman architecture, a scroll shaped decoration used at the top of a column.

_____ 5. Large leaves used by the Greeks in the decoration of architecture and artwork.

_____ 6. A motif used on furniture resembling a fan-shaped palm branch.

_____ 7. Lacelike patterns cut in stone on Gothic architecture.

_____ 8. Parallel grooves used to ornament a surface.

_____ 9. A furniture foot with the same shape as a spade foot.

_____ 10. An ornamentation used on furniture legs made by rotating wood on a lathe and shaping with cutting tools.

Column B

A. acanthus leaves

B. bun foot

C. Flemish foot

D. fluting

E. Gothic tracery

F. Ionic capital

G. palmette

H. thimble foot

I. trestle

J. turning

Traditional French Furniture
Activity 11-2

Name _____

Date _____

Describe the dominant features of each Traditional furniture styles from France listed below.

1. Late Renaissance (1589–1643): _____

_____

_____

_____

_____

2. Baroque (1643–1700): _____

_____

_____

_____

_____

3. Regence (1700–1730): _____

_____

_____

_____

_____

4. Rococo (1730–1760): _____

_____

_____

_____

_____

5. Neoclassic (1760–1789): _____

_____

_____

_____

_____

6. Directoire (1789–1804): _____

_____

_____

_____

_____

7. Empire (1804–1820): _____

_____

_____

_____

_____

Traditional English Furniture
Activity 11-3

Name _____

Date _____

Identify each of the English furniture pieces, architectural details, or designs from the Early and Middle Renaissance periods. Write the style and dates below each illustration.

1. _____

    _____

2. _____

    _____

3. _____

    _____

4. _____

    _____

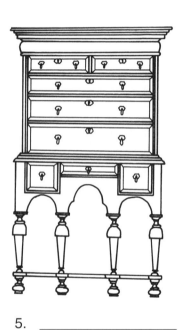

5. _____

    _____

6. _____

    _____

7. _____

    _____

8. _____

    _____

English Furniture
Activity 11-4

Name _____

Date _____

Identify each Late Georgian furniture piece by the cabinetmaker or designer who produced it and list key features about the piece. England's master cabinetmakers and prominent designers during the Late Georgian period were Thomas Chippendale, George Hepplewhite, Thomas Sheraton, and Robert and James Adam.

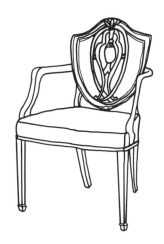

1. _____
_____
_____
_____

2. _____
_____
_____
_____

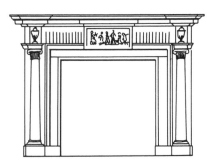

3. _____
_____
_____
_____

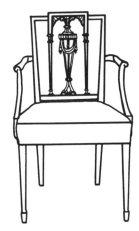

4. _____
_____
_____
_____

Traditional American Furniture
Activity 11-5

Name _____

Date _____

Each furniture piece shown below is representative of a traditional American style. Identify the description that best describes each drawing and write its initial in the space provided.

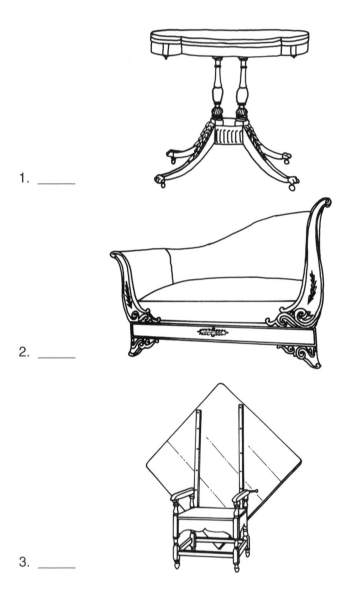

1. _____

A. **Early American (1630–1770):** Furniture was mostly patterned after English Gothic and Jacobean styles. Tables were plain, and chairs were straight and upright with flat or caned seats. Furniture decoration included split spindles, turnings, and bun feet. Geometric or floral patterns were carved in low relief.

2. _____

B. **American Georgian (1720–1790):** Chairs were contoured to fit the human form. The wing chair became popular. Slender, turned legs that slanted outward were used. The secretary chest became popular as well as highboys and lowboys with brass hardware.

3. _____

C. **Federal (1790–1820):** Furniture was delicate and of excellent proportions. Ornamentation was patriotic in nature. The eagle was popular as well as cornucopias, fruit, flowers, and spiral turnings. Duncan Phyfe was considered the outstanding cabinetmaker of the Federal period.

4. _____

D. **Post Federal (1820–1880):** From 1820 to 1840, the American Empire style was popular, featuring furniture of heavy proportions. From 1840 to 1880, American designs were patterned after English Victorian styles. Designs were adapted to mechanization.

Brick Veneer Walls
Activity 13-2

Name _____

Date _____

Using the following terms, label each of the components indicated in the brick-veneer-on-frame wall below.

flashing   metal tie   stud

foundation   sheathing   subfloor

joist   sill

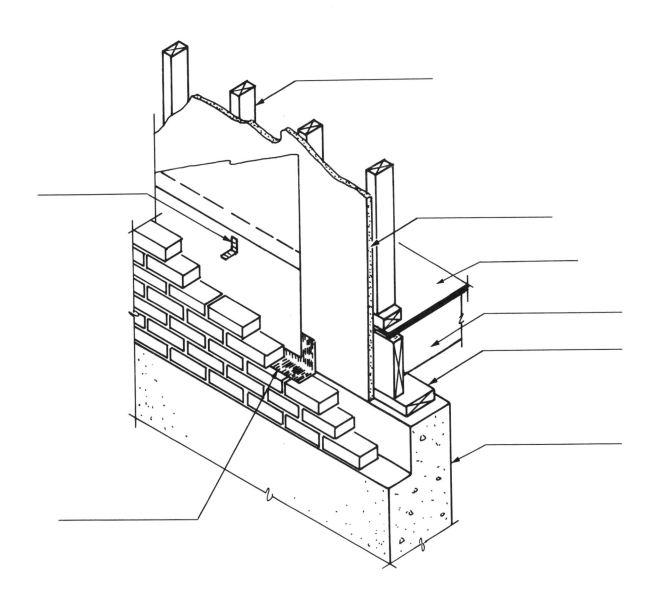

Basement Walls
Activity 13-3

Name _____

Date _____

Using the following terms, label each part of the basement/foundation wall and floor system below.

basement floor
concrete block wall
drain tile

expansion joint
parging

pea gravel
reinforcing rods

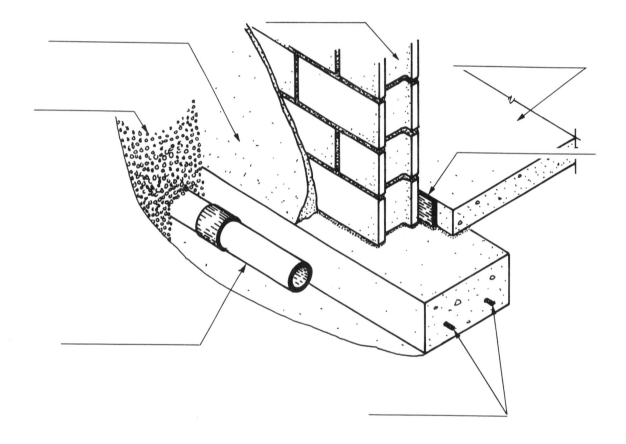

Exterior Wall Materials
Activity 13-4

Name _____

Date _____

In each space below, sketch an elevation view of the indicated exterior wall material. Try to approximate the proper size of the materials, assuming the scale is ½ in. = 1 ft.

1. 6 in. horizontal wood siding

2. 8 by 16 in. concrete block

3. 2 by 8 in. common brick

4. Stucco

5. Board and batten

6. Coursed stone

7. 12 by 12 in. glass block

8. Cedar shingles

Interior Walls
Activity 13-5

Name _____

Date _____

Plan the interior wall treatment and trim for a family room that includes the following: painted facings and wood trim; wallpaper; and a textured ceiling covered with a white, flat finish. Mount the paint and wallpaper samples in the spaces below. Specify the name, number, type, and manufacturer of each.

Mount wallpaper sample here.

_____

_____

Mount trim-paint
color sample here.

Mount ceiling-paint
color sample here.

_____

_____

_____

_____

Interior Wall Treatments
Activity 13-6

Name _____

Date _____

Compare the costs of covering a 4 by 8 ft. area with quality versions of the interior wall treatments listed below. Describe each type of treatment by identifying the product's name, price, and manufacturer, as well as the store at which it can be purchased and a rough estimate of the installed price.

1. Clear redwood boards: _____

_____

_____

_____

_____

_____

_____

2. Hardwood paneling: _____

_____

_____

_____

_____

_____

_____

3. Ceramic tile: _____

_____

_____

_____

_____

_____

_____

4. Wallpaper:_____

_____

_____

_____

_____

_____

_____

Wall Decoration
Activity 13-7

Name _____

Date _____

Select a picture from a magazine that you believe applies the principles of good design to wall areas. Mount it below and discuss the good points of the design.

Mount picture here.

This is an example of good design for a wall area because _____

_____

_____

_____

_____

_____

_____

_____

_____

_____

_____

_____

Wood Floor Patterns
Activity 14-4

Name _____

Date _____

A new, modular wood flooring material is produced in a standard width of 4½ in. and lengths of 9, 18, 27, and 36 in. Plan four patterns using any combination of these standard modular pieces. (Each square in the design grids below is 4½ by 4½ in.)

1.
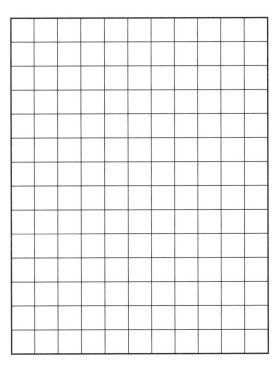

2.
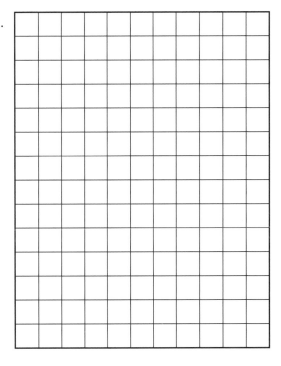

3.

4.

Flooring Materials
Activity 14-5

Name _____

Date _____

In each space below, draw a plan view of the flooring material indicated. The scale is *1 in. = 1 ft.*

1. 2 by 2 in. ceramic mosaic tile

2. 6 by 6 in. quarry tile

3. 4 by 6 in. brick pavers

4. Random rectangular slate

5. Flagstone

6. Terrazzo

Floor-Area Design
Activity 14-8

Name _____

Date _____

Select a picture from a magazine that applies the principles of good design to the interior floor of a home. Mount the picture in the space below and describe the good points of the design.

Mount picture here.

This is an example of good floor design because _____

_____

_____

_____

_____

_____

_____

_____

_____

_____

_____

_____

Chapter 15
Ceilings and Roofs

Check Your Understanding

Name _____

Date _____

Short Answer: Provide brief answers to the following questions or statements.

1. List two advantages of lower ceiling heights. _____
   _____
   _____

2. What is the difference between ceiling and floor joists? _____
   _____
   _____
   _____

3. Why are suspended ceilings useful for work or grooming areas? _____
   _____
   _____

4. List two characteristics of highly textured ceilings. _____
   _____
   _____

5. What type of ceiling treatment would be appropriate for a game room when reducing noise is a factor? _____
   _____
   _____

6. What type of cornice is likely to be found on a cabin's exterior? _____
   _____

7. Identify at least four types of roof sheathing materials. _____
   _____
   _____
   _____
   _____

(continued)

Name _____

Date _____

8. What is flashing and why is it used? _____

_____

_____

9. What purpose do gutters and downspouts serve? _____

_____

_____

10. Why is ventilation necessary in roofs? Where may vents be placed? _____

_____

_____

_____

_____

_____

11. How does the roof covering on a flat roof differ from that on most other types of roofs? _____

_____

_____

12. Why is it important to know in the early stages of house design what type of roofing material will
    be used? _____

_____

_____

Completion: Complete the following sentences by writing the missing words in the preceding blanks.

_____ 13. A type of ceiling with exposed beams and a surface covering that is
                                 attached to the rafters is a _____ ceiling.

_____ 14. The most commonly used ceiling surface material is _____ board.

_____ 15. A base material to which plaster is applied is _____.

_____ 16. The first coat of a plaster finish applied directly to the base material is
                                 the _____ coat.

_____ 17. The second coat of a three-coat plaster finish is the _____ coat.

_____ 18. A type of ceiling treatment that is easy to apply and provides a passive
                                 background is _____.

_____ 19. The structural base of the roof surface is formed by the _____.

_____ 20. The highest horizontal line at which two sections of a roof meet is the

                                 _____.

_____ 21. The angular intersection formed by sections of the roof that slope down
                                 from the ridge is called the _____.

(continued)

Name _____

Date _____

_____ 22. The vertical distance of a roof measured from the top of the wall plate to the underside of the rafters is the _____.

_____ 23. One-half the distance of the clear span of a roof is the _____.

_____ 24. Distance from the outside of one exterior wall to the outside of the opposite exterior wall is the _____.

_____ 25. The overhanging area of a roof is the _____.

_____ 26. The underside of the cornice is the _____.

_____ 27. A part of the roof that extends horizontally past the end walls of the house are _____ ends, or rakes.

_____ 28. The type of roof often called the barn roof is the _____ roof.

_____ 29. A type of roofing material applied in strips is _____ roofing.

Ceiling Types
Activity 15-1

Name _____

Date _____

The illustrations below show four common types of ceiling surfaces attached to ceiling joists. In the space provided, identify the primary qualities and/or considerations for each type of ceiling.

1.

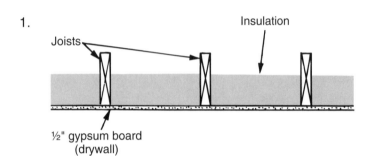

Joists

Insulation

½" gypsum board
(drywall)

Important Qualities/Considerations

_____
_____
_____
_____
_____
_____

2.

Plaster   Wire lath

Important Qualities/Considerations

_____
_____
_____
_____
_____
_____

3.

Board paneling

Important Qualities/Considerations

_____
_____
_____
_____
_____
_____

4.

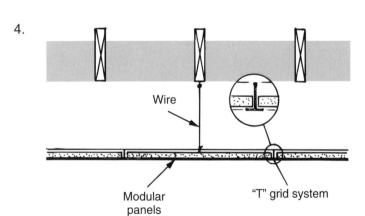

Wire

Modular
panels

"T" grid system

Important Qualities/Considerations

_____
_____
_____
_____
_____
_____

Ceiling Treatments
Activity 15-2

Name _____

Date _____

Plan the ceiling treatment for the family room below. Choose either paint, textured plaster, or a suspended ceiling with 2 ft. sq. panels. The ceiling now has a drywall surface that is ready for a primer coat of paint. Record the total area of the ceiling plus the materials required and their individual costs. Then calculate the total cost of materials for the ceiling treatment.

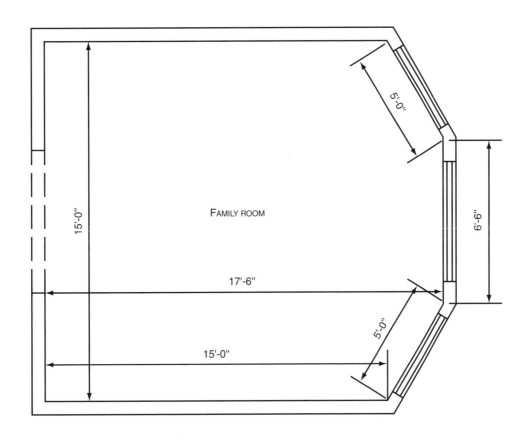

Total ceiling area: _____

Materials required: (Specify the cost of each.) _____

_____

_____

_____

_____

_____

_____

Total cost of materials: _____

Roofs
Activity 15-3

Name _____

Date _____

Identify each of the common roof styles shown below. Then match each description in Column A with the correct roof style in Column B. Place the appropriate letter in each blank.

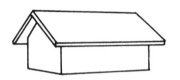

1. _____

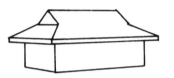

2. _____

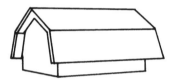

3. _____

4. _____

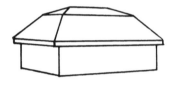

5. _____

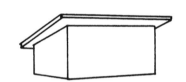

6. _____

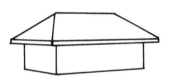

7. _____

Column A

_____ 8. One of the most economical roofs to build. Not covered with traditional roofing materials.

_____ 9. Is much more complex to build than the gable or hip roof. Provides extra space on the top floor.

_____ 10. More complicated than the gable roof. Provides a cornice on all four sides of the house. Does not provide good ventilation.

_____ 11. One of the most popular residential roof styles. Is simple and economical to build. Allows good ventilation.

_____ 12. Has a gable added to each end of the hip. Creates an interesting roof line. Provides for ventilation.

_____ 13. Has more slope than a flat roof. Requires a built-up roof covering if the slope is less than 3:12.

_____ 14. Often called a barn roof. Common on Dutch Colonial style homes. Permits added headroom on the top level of the house.

Column B

A. Dutch hip

B. flat

C. gable

D. gambrel

E. hip

F. Mansard

G. shed

Roofing Materials
Activity 15-4

Name _____

Date _____

Describe the qualities of the roofing materials listed below, including the basic factors that are important for a homeowner to consider.

1. Asphalt roofing: _____

_____

_____

_____

_____

_____

_____

2. Wood shingles and shakes: _____

_____

_____

_____

_____

_____

_____

3. Tile, slate, and concrete materials: _____

_____

_____

_____

_____

_____

4. Metal: _____

_____

_____

_____

_____

_____

_____

Window Sizes
Activity 16-2

Name _____

Date _____

Select a window style that appeals to you. Find a picture, photo, or drawing of the window in a typical housing application. Using manufacturer's literature, specify common sizes for the rough opening. Attach details about the construction of the window.

Place picture of window here.

Common Sizes

_____   _____   _____

_____   _____   _____

_____   _____   _____

_____   _____   _____

_____   _____   _____

Window Features
Activity 16-3

Name _____

Date _____

Describe each of the window-related features and materials below. Be sure to include information that would interest a housing designer.

1. Wood window frame: _____
    _____
    _____
    _____

2. Aluminum window frame: _____
    _____
    _____
    _____

3. Vinyl clad wood frame: _____
    _____
    _____
    _____

4. Metal clad wood frame: _____
    _____
    _____
    _____

5. Vinyl window frame: _____
    _____
    _____
    _____

6. Single paned glass window: _____
    _____
    _____
    _____

7. Insulating glass window: _____
    _____
    _____
    _____

8. Reflective coatings: _____
    _____
    _____

Window Placement
Activity 16-4

Name _____

Date _____

Study the size and placement of windows in the bedroom plan below. In the bottom illustration, indicate how you would change window placement and size to gain better airflow and room use.

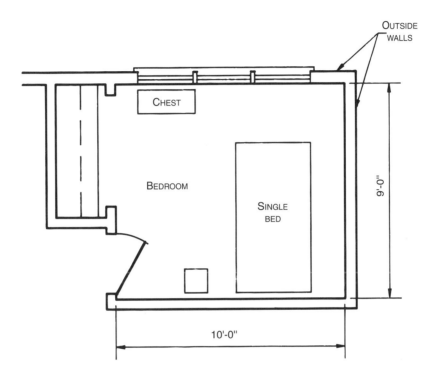

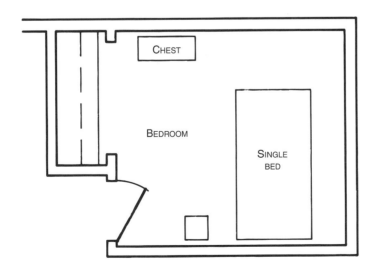

Interior Window Treatments
Activity 16-5

Name _____

Date _____

Sketch each window treatment named below. Each sketch should reflect proper proportion and placement of the treatment to the respective window.

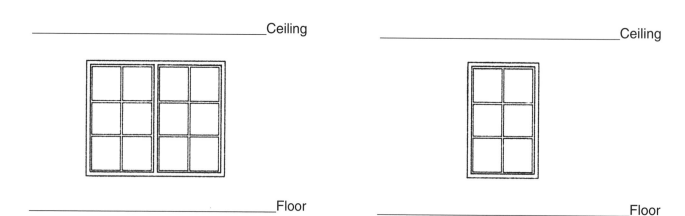

_____Ceiling

_____Floor

1.   Floor-length draperies on a decorative rod

_____Ceiling

_____Floor

3.   Cafe curtains

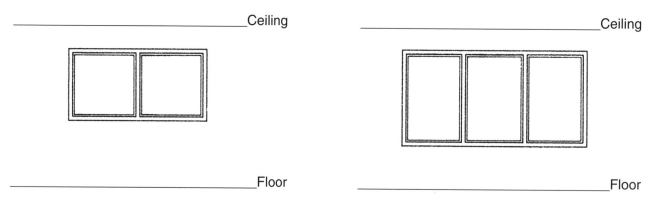

_____Ceiling

_____Floor

2.   Draperies with a cornice or valance

_____Ceiling

_____Floor

4.   Roman shades

Door Symbols
Activity 16-6

Name _____

Date _____

For each of the residential door types named and shown below, draw the symbol used in construction drawings under its illustration.

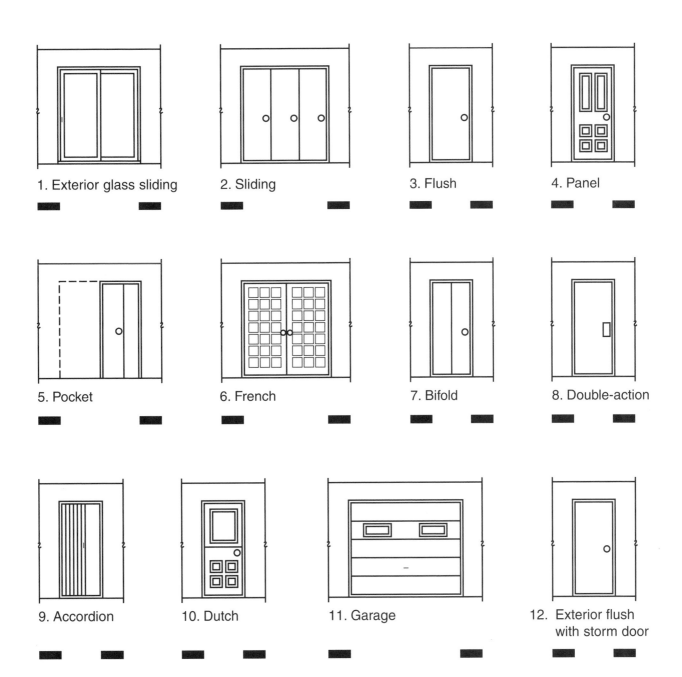

1. Exterior glass sliding

2. Sliding

3. Flush

4. Panel

5. Pocket

6. French

7. Bifold

8. Double-action

9. Accordion

10. Dutch

11. Garage

12. Exterior flush with storm door

Door Applications
Activity 16-7

Name _____

Date _____

On the floor plan below, sketch door symbols in appropriate locations for the following types of doors: accordion, bifold, flush, French, pocket, and sliding. Label each door symbol.

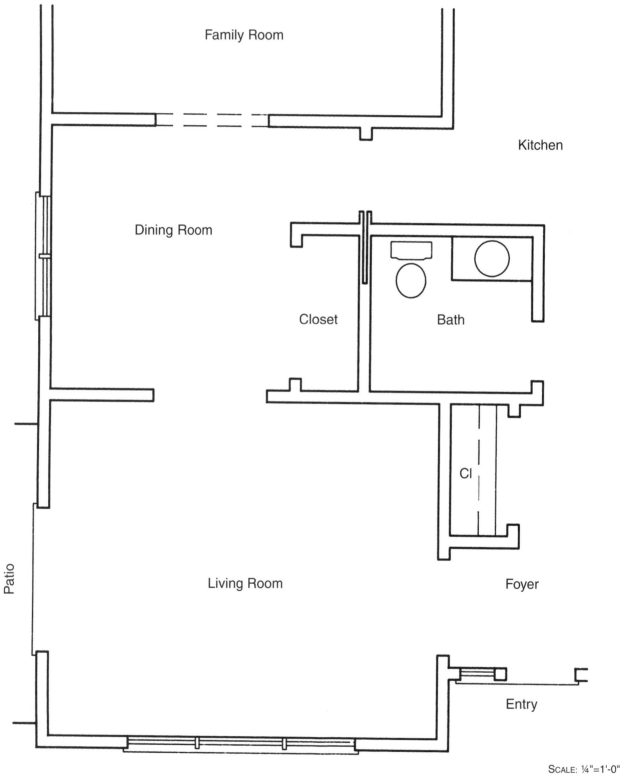

SCALE: ¼"=1'-0"

Chapter 17
Stairs and Halls

Check Your Understanding

Name _____

Date _____

Matching: Match the stairway descriptions in Column A with the terms in Column B. Place the appropriate letter in each blank.

Column A

_____ 1. Two flights of steps parallel to each other with one landing between them.

_____ 2. A flat floor area that may be used at any point along a staircase.

_____ 3. Horizontal member of each step.

_____ 4. Wedge-shaped steps that are substituted for a landing.

_____ 5. Series of steps that lead from one level to another in a structure.

_____ 6. Several wedge-shaped steps fastened together to form a cylindrical stairway.

_____ 7. The usually rounded projection of a stair tread that extends past the face of the riser below.

_____ 8. Stairway with no turns or landings midway.

_____ 9. Two landings along a stair flight, facing in opposite directions, each with a 90° turn.

_____ 10. Uses trapezoid-shaped steps.

_____ 11. Changes direction and includes one landing.

Column B

A. circular stairs

B. double-L stairs

C. L stairs

D. landing

E. nosing

F. spiral stairs

G. stairway

H. straight-run stairs

I. tread

J. U stairs

K. winder stairs

Short Answer: Provide brief answers to the following questions or statements.

12. How do main and service stairways differ in use, type of construction, and materials? _____

_____

_____

_____

_____

_____

_____

(continued)

Name _____

Date _____

13. Which type of stairs is the easiest and most economical to build? _____

_____

14. Which type of stairs is generally considered unsafe because of varying widths of treads? _____

_____

15. Which type of stairs is ideal for a house with little stairway space? _____

_____

16. Which type of stairs uses an arc or irregular curve as its basic shape? _____

_____

17. What safety considerations should be given to risers and treads? _____

_____

_____

18. Should all types of stairs be the same width? Explain. _____

_____

_____

19. What is the ideal length and placement of a handrail? _____

_____

_____

_____

20. How can you determine if a specific house plan has the proper amount of headroom for the stairs?

_____

_____

_____

21. What should be considered when planning the decorating scheme for a stairway? _____

_____

_____

_____

_____

_____

22. If carpeting is planned for a stairway, what type is best? _____

_____

_____

_____

(continued)

Name_____

Date _____

23. For a long hallway that provides access to four bedrooms and an office, how wide should it be?

_____

_____

24. For a hallway, is a tightly woven tan carpet with short pile or a white sculptured carpet generally the better choice? Why? _____

_____

_____

_____

_____

_____

_____

25. What should be considered when choosing wall treatments for hallways? _____

_____

_____

_____

_____

_____

_____

Stair Designs
Activity 17-1

Name _____

Date _____

Identify each type of stairway illustrated below. Write the correct names on the lines provided.

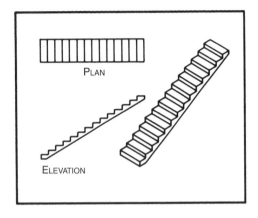

1. _____

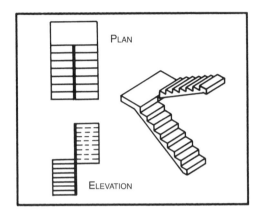

2. _____

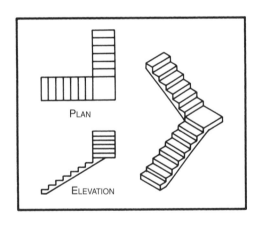

3. _____

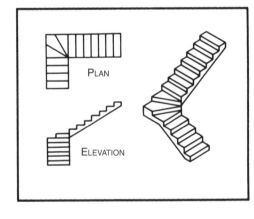

4. _____

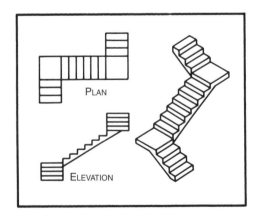

5. _____

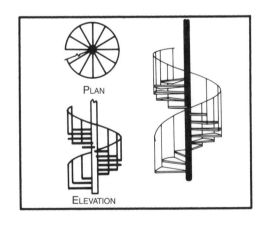

6. _____

Stair Specifications
Activity 17-2

Name _____

Date _____

Analyze the data from four main stairways in terms of recommended design principles. Specify the items that fail to meet the accepted stairway design standards recommended in your text.

Stairway #1

    Riser height: 7¼ in.
    Run of a step: 10½ in.
    Slope of the stairs: 34½°
    Width of the stairs: 34 in.
    Handrail height: 36 in.
    Headroom of stairs: 6 ft. 6 in.

Unacceptable specifications:

_____

_____

_____

_____

_____

_____

_____

_____

Stairway #2

    Riser height: 8¼ in.
    Run of a step: 10½ in.
    Slope of the stairs: 38°
    Width of the stairs: 42 in.
    Handrail height: 30 in.
    Headroom of stairs: 6 ft. 8 in.

Unacceptable specifications:

_____

_____

_____

_____

_____

_____

_____

_____

Stairway #3

    Riser height: 7 in.
    Run of a step: 11 in.
    Slope of the stairs: 32½°
    Width of the stairs: 34 in.
    Handrail height: 34 in.
    Headroom of stairs: 6 ft. 4 in.

Unacceptable specifications:

_____

_____

_____

_____

_____

_____

_____

_____

Stairway #4

    Riser height: 7⅛ in.
    Run of a step: 9¾ in.
    Slope of the stairs: 36¼°
    Width of the stairs: 36 in.
    Handrail height: 30 in.
    Headroom of stairs: 6 ft. 6 in.

Unacceptable specifications:

_____

_____

_____

_____

_____

_____

_____

_____

Hall Space
Activity 17-3

Name _____

Date _____

Study the floor plan, examining the hallway and other circulation space. Then evaluate the amount, configuration, and location of the circulation space in this plan.

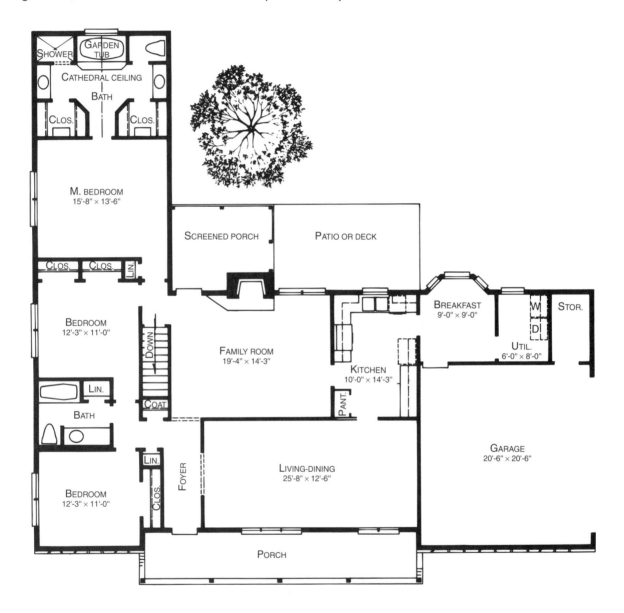

Amount of circulation space: _____

_____

_____

_____

_____

_____

Name _____

Date _____

Configuration of circulation space: _____

_____

_____

_____

_____

_____

_____

_____

_____

_____

_____

_____

_____

_____

_____

_____

_____

_____

_____

_____

_____

_____

_____

_____

_____

_____

_____

_____

_____

_____

_____

_____

_____

_____

(continued)

Name _____

Date _____

Location of circulation space: _____

_____

_____

_____

_____

_____

_____

_____

_____

_____

_____

_____

_____

_____

_____

_____

_____

_____

_____

_____

_____

_____

_____

_____

_____

_____

_____

_____

_____

_____

_____

_____

_____

_____

_____

_____

_____

_____

_____

Lighting Application
Activity 18-5

Name _____

Date _____

Plan the lighting for the grand foyer shown below. The activities anticipated in this area include reading as well as meeting and greeting guests. Describe your plan in the space provided. Note: The ceiling is vaulted over the center section of the foyer area.

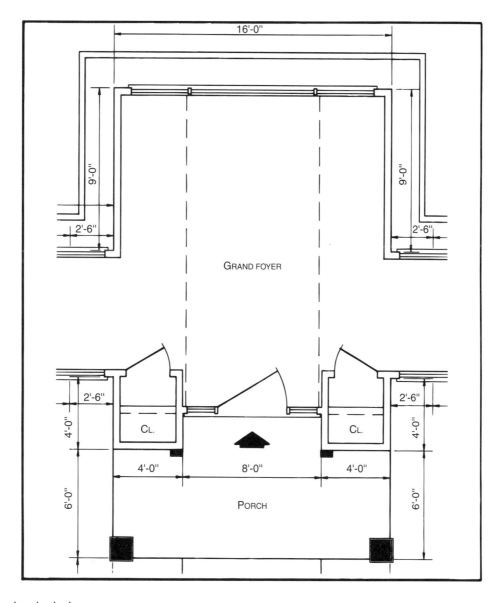

The lighting plan includes: _____

_____

_____

_____

_____

(continued)

Name _____

Date _____

Chapter 19
Electrical and Plumbing Systems

Check Your Understanding

Name _____

Date _____

Matching: Match the descriptions in Column A with the terms in Column B. Place the appropriate letter in each blank.

Column A

_____ 1. Controls a light fixture from one location.

_____ 2. Includes sinks, shower stalls, and water closets.

_____ 3. Prevents excessive flow of current in a circuit.

_____ 4. Prevents gases from entering the living space.

_____ 5. Designed for outdoor use.

_____ 6. Permits water and waste to drain away and gases to vent outside.

_____ 7. Used with two electrical conductors.

_____ 8. Refers to ground fault circuit interrupter.

_____ 9. Provides an appropriate amount of current.

_____ 10. Contains mercury or a spring to connect and break the circuit.

_____ 11. Accommodates four receptacles.

_____ 12. Powered by a 120-volt circuit with a 20-ampere capacity.

_____ 13. Accommodates three receptacles.

_____ 14. Brings the water supply from the city main or private well to the dwelling.

_____ 15. Accommodates one receptacle.

Column B

A. 120-volt service

B. branch circuit

C. building main

D. GFCI

E. handle-type switch

F. overcurrent device

G. plumbing fixtures

H. quad

I. simplex

J. single-pole switch

K. small-appliance circuit

L. soil stack

M. trap

N. triplex

O. waterproof receptacle

Short Answer: Provide brief answers to the following questions or statements.

16. What is the function of the service-entrance panel? _____

_____

_____

(continued)

Name _____

Date _____

17. How do small-appliance circuits differ from individual-appliance circuits? _____

_____

_____

_____

_____

_____

_____

18. What is the difference between receptacles with grounding terminals versus without? _____

_____

_____

_____

_____

19. What is low-voltage switching and why is it becoming more popular? _____

_____

_____

_____

_____

_____

20. What factors should be considered when planning the electrical system for a home? _____

_____

_____

_____

_____

_____

_____

21. Trace the main parts of the cold water supply, beginning at the city water main or private well.

_____

_____

_____

_____

(continued)

Name _____

Date _____

22. Compare the size, materials used, and function of pipes in the water supply system to those in the wastewater removal system. _____

_____

_____

_____

_____

_____

_____

_____

23. To reduce costs when planning a structure's plumbing system, what factors should be considered?

_____

_____

_____

24. What is the proper size water heater for a five-person household with two bathrooms, a clothes washer, and an automatic dishwasher? _____

_____

25. What three functions does a home signal and communication system perform? _____

_____

_____

_____

Completion: Complete the following sentences by writing the missing words in the preceding blanks.

_____ 26. Power is supplied to a circuit branch by fuses or _____.

_____ 27. Three power lines leading into a service-entrance panel indicate that _____-volt service is available.

_____ 28. Power is supplied to lighting fixtures and receptacles by a _____ -volt circuit.

_____ 29. The National Electrical Code requires at least _____ separate small-appliance circuits for each kitchen.

_____ 30. The _____ appliance circuit is needed for any permanent, motor-driven appliance requiring over 1,440 watts to operate.

_____ 31. Bathrooms and areas around pools should have GFCI receptacles to protect against _____ from a short in an appliance.

_____ 32. To control a fixture from two locations requires the installation of a _____ -way switch.

(continued)

Name _____

Date _____

_____ 33. Switches that use a rocker-type mechanism for operations are _____ switches.

_____ 34. Having one general-purpose circuit for no more than _____ sq. ft. is a safe, practical guideline for modern homes.

_____ 35. Each frequently used room entrance requires a _____ switch to prevent entering a darkened room.

_____ 36. A functional arrangement for planning receptacles is to place them at _____ ft. intervals.

_____ 37. Receptacles are generally placed _____ to 18 in. above the floor.

Electrical Circuits
Activity 19-1

Name _____

Date _____

Use the following terms to identify the components of the simple residential electrical system illustrated below.

bathroom heater	kitchen	service-entrance panel
clocks	lamps	small-appliance circuits
dryer	receptacles	water heater
electric range	separate oven	workshop

(Destination)

(Type of Circuit)

General-Purpose Circuits

1,800 watts

1,800 watts

1,800 watts

2,400 watts

2,400 watts

Individual-Appliance Circuits

12,000 watts

5,000 watts

2,000 watts

5,000 watts

5,000 watts

Receptacles and Switches
Activity 19-2

Name _____

Date _____

Use the following terms to identify the specific type of receptacle or switch described below.

240-volt receptacle
clock receptacle
dimmer switch
duplex receptacle

four-way switch
GFCI receptacle
pull-chain switch
simplex receptacle

single-pole switch
three-way switch
weatherproof receptacle

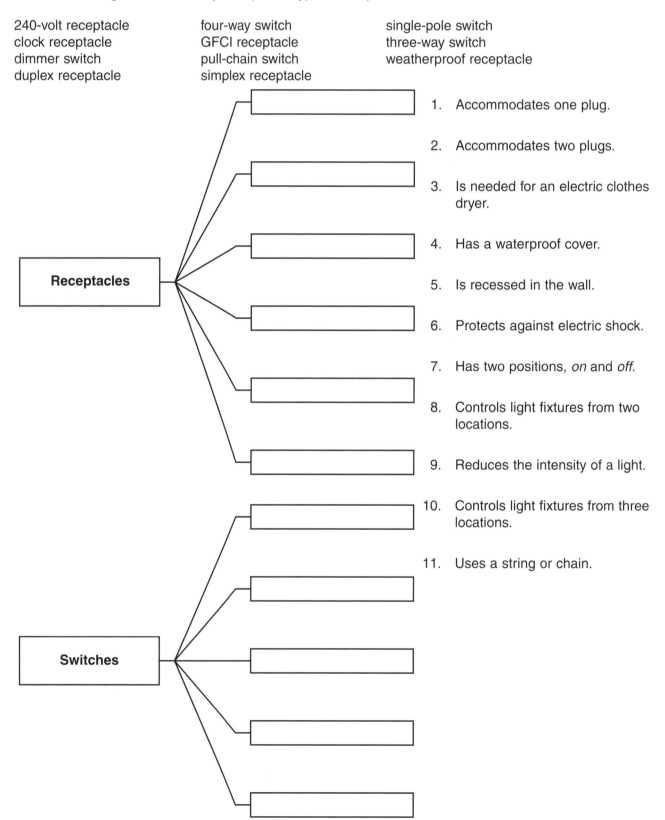

Receptacles

Switches

1. Accommodates one plug.

2. Accommodates two plugs.

3. Is needed for an electric clothes dryer.

4. Has a waterproof cover.

5. Is recessed in the wall.

6. Protects against electric shock.

7. Has two positions, *on* and *off.*

8. Controls light fixtures from two locations.

9. Reduces the intensity of a light.

10. Controls light fixtures from three locations.

11. Uses a string or chain.

Electrical Plan
Activity 19-3

Name _____

Date _____

Plan the receptacles and switches for the room shown below. Sketch or draw in the symbols and then fill in the National Electrical Code circuit requirements in the spaces provided.

22'-0"

18'-0"

WORK BENCH

10"
TABLE SAW

WINDOW
AIR CONDITIONER

12"
BANDSAW

6"
GRINDER

6"
DRILL PRESS

General-purpose circuits: Number _____   Watts per circuit _____

Small-appliance circuits: Number _____   Watts per circuit _____

Individual-appliance circuits: _____

_____

_____

_____

_____

Plumbing System
Activity 19-4

Name _____

Date _____

Use the following terms to identify the parts of the residential plumbing system illustrated schematically below. Some words may be used more than once.

building main
cold water main
fixtures
hot water main

house drain
house sewer
plumbing fixtures
soil stack

water heater
water main (or well)
water softener

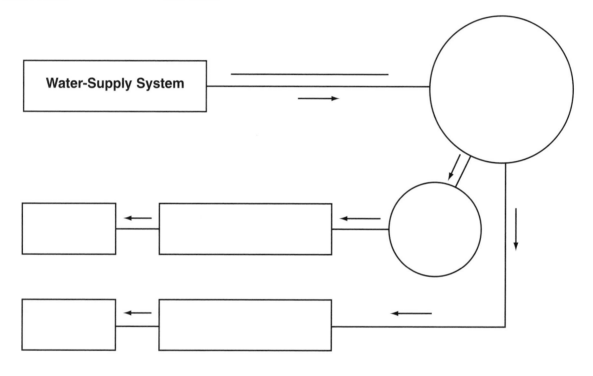

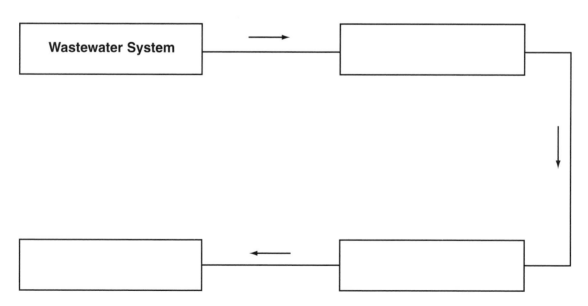

Chapter 20
Climate Control, Fireplaces, and Stoves

Check Your Understanding

Name _____

Date _____

Short Answer: Provide brief answers to the following questions or statements.

1. Why does the forced warm-air heating system require two sets of ducts? _____

_____

_____

_____

2. Why are water wells sometimes used in central heat-pump systems? _____

_____

_____

_____

3. How many cubic feet of stone are needed to provide storage for heat collected by three 4 by 8 ft. solar collectors? How many cubic feet of water storage are needed for the same amount of collector space? _____

_____

_____

4. What types of heating systems are *not* recommended for cold climates unless a backup system is installed?_____

_____

_____

_____

5. List the benefits of a cooling system. _____

_____

_____

6. Name the four materials commonly used for insulation. _____

_____

_____

_____

_____

(continued)

Name _____

Date _____

7. What are the indications of low humidity? _____

_____

_____

8. What features make prefabricated heat-circulating fireplaces more efficient than traditional fireplaces?

_____

_____

_____

_____

9. Which type of stove provides more safety for a family with very young children? _____

_____

10. How can the efficiency of a stove be increased when it is located in front of an existing fireplace?

_____

_____

Multiple Choice: Select the best response and write the letter in the preceding blank.

_____   11. Advantages of a forced warm-air system include _____.
                 A. quiet operation
                 B. easy and inexpensive installation
                 C. quick heat
                 D. All of the above.

_____   12. The advantages of a central heat pump include _____.
                 A. no chimney required
                 B. use of very little space indoors
                 C. a combined heating and cooling unit
                 D. All of the above.

_____   13. Factors that determine the number of registers required in a room for a forced warm-air
                 heating system include _____.
                 A. room size
                 B. expected heat loss
                 C. desired room temperature
                 D. All of the above.

_____   14. Absorber plates used in active solar systems are covered with _____ to absorb as much
                 energy as possible.
                 A. textured black coating
                 B. shiny black coating
                 C. flat black coating
                 D. foiled black coating

(continued)

Name _____

Date _____

_____ 15. The compressor-cycle cooling system uses _____ to cool the air.
A. solar collectors
B. blowers
C. chemical refrigerant
D. heat pumps

_____ 16. A cooling system is easily attached to the _____ because the same ducts are used.
A. hydronic system
B. electric radiant system
C. passive solar system
D. forced warm-air system

_____ 17. A material having a high R-value is _____.
A. expanded polystyrene
B. glass
C. concrete
D. common brick

_____ 18. The part of a fireplace that controls the burning rate and prevents downdrafts of cold air is the _____.
A. smoke shelf
B. flue
C. firebox
D. damper

_____ 19. High-efficiency stoves have features that include _____.
A. good control of the amount of primary and secondary air used for combustion
B. baffles, long smoke paths, and heat exchange devices to increase heat output
C. Both of the above.
D. None of the above.

Completion: Complete the following sentences by writing the missing words in the preceding blanks.

_____ 20. Furnaces generally use natural gas or _____ for fuel.

_____ 21. The amount of heat delivered to a heating space is controlled by the _____.

_____ 22. A hydronic system delivers heat to a home through copper tubing embedded in the floor, radiant panels, or _____.

_____ 23. Solar collectors have _____ plates that are heated by the rays of the sun.

_____ 24. Active solar systems need an area large enough to store heat required for _____ days of cloudy weather.

_____ 25. The level of resistance to _____ is designated as the R-value.

_____ 26. The amount of moisture in the air is _____.

_____ 27. A total climate-control system involves temperature and humidity control as well as air circulation and _____.

_____ 28. The upward flow of air in a fireplace to draw sufficient oxygen and thus help a fire burn well is the _____.

_____ 29. Stoves generally use coal or _____ as fuel.

Heating Systems
Activity 20-1

Name _____

Date _____

In the space provided, describe the components of the heating systems named below and explain how each delivers heat to the home.

1. Forced warm-air systems: _____

   _____

   _____

   _____

   _____

2. Hydronic systems: _____

   _____

   _____

   _____

   _____

3. Electric radiant systems: _____

   _____

   _____

   _____

   _____

4. Central heat-pump systems: _____

   _____

   _____

   _____

   _____

5. Active solar heating systems: _____

   _____

   _____

   _____

   _____

6. Passive solar heating systems: _____

   _____

   _____

   _____

Masonry Fireplace
Activity 20-2

Name _____

Date _____

Use the following terms to identify the parts of the typical masonry fireplace shown below.

angle steel lintel	clean-out door	fire stop	mantle
ash dump	concrete slab	flashing	outer hearth
basement floor	damper	flue lining	smoke chamber
cap	firebrick	footing	smoke shelf

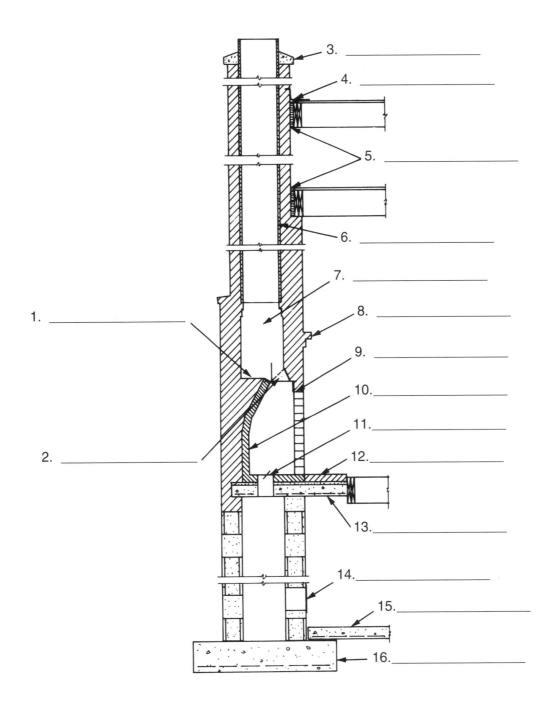

3. _____

4. _____

5. _____

6. _____

7. _____

1. _____

8. _____

9. _____

10. _____

11. _____

2. _____

12. _____

13. _____

14. _____

15. _____

16. _____

Chapter 21
Communication, Security, and Home Automation

Check Your Understanding

Name _____

Date _____

Matching: Match the descriptions in Column A with the terms in Column B. Place the appropriate letter in each blank.

Column A

_____ 1. Electrically operated switches.

_____ 2. The two wires of a telephone line.

_____ 3. Provides access to digital video services.

_____ 4. Devices that supply the electrical power to doorbells, chimes, signal lights, or warning devices.

_____ 5. More commonly used in commercial security and surveillance activities than in home systems.

_____ 6. The final line of defense for home security systems.

_____ 7. Sends a silent alarm to a monitoring station.

_____ 8. The central hub of a structured wiring installation.

Column B

A. cable pair

B. hard-wired systems

C. motion detectors

D. panic button

E. relays

F. RG-6 cable

G. signaling circuits

H. wiring closet

Completion: Complete the following sentences by writing the missing words in the preceding blanks.

_____ 9. Devices that perform _____ functions initiate an action based on an input.

_____ 10. A minimum of _____ standard telephone lines are recommended for new homes.

_____ 11. A safety and security concern that should be included in the overall security strategy is _____ detection.

_____ 12. For cost-effective property protection, consumers frequently protect only the _____ and rely on motion detectors to warn of intruders.

_____ 13. The first line of defense in a security system designed to protect the occupants as well as the property is a _____ system.

_____ 14. The earliest warning of fire in a home security system is a _____ detector.

_____ 15. The ability of products to "talk" and "listen" to one another is an example of _____.

_____ 16. A protocol called _____ is associated with power line technology.

_____ 17. The wiring in a structured wiring system generally consists of _____ cable.

_____ 18. Bundled cable has several conductors inside one _____ jacket.

_____ 19. Another name for low-voltage switching is _____ _____ wiring.

(continued)

Name _____

Date _____

Multiple Choice: Select the best response and write the letter in the preceding blanks.

_____ 20. Which of the following functions is *not* a part of new technology systems for residential construction?
A. monitoring functions
B. networking functions
C. switching functions
D. programming functions

_____ 21. Conditions that may be monitored in a home include _____.
A. sound within the home
B. window and door status
C. carbon monoxide levels
D. All of the above.

_____ 22. A typical telephone line may be used for _____.
A. information transfer and communication
B. conversation only
C. video and audio transmission
D. satellite transmission

_____ 23. A device that senses movement or body heat in a home is a _____.
A. smoke detector
B. glassbreak detector
C. passive infared (PIR) or motion sensor
D. shock sensor

_____ 24. A perimeter security system is controlled by a _____.
A. TV monitor
B. key pad
C. digitizing tablet
D. panic button

_____ 25. An open network standard for home automation systems is _____.
A. Consumer Electronic Bus (CEBus)
B. Smart House®
C. LONWorks®
D. All of the above.

Types of System Functions
Activity 21-1

Name _____

Date _____

Match the descriptions in Column A with the terms in Column B. Place the appropriate letter in each blank. (Letters may be used more than once.)

Column A

_____ 1. Alerting a homeowner to potential danger.

_____ 2. Allowing live video and data communication.

_____ 3. Detecting smoke levels.

_____ 4. Directing the entertainment system to record a favorite program every day.

_____ 5. Distinguishing humidity levels.

_____ 6. Doing research on the Internet.

_____ 7. Identifying movement within the house.

_____ 8. Locking or unlocking doors, windows, and vents.

_____ 9. Opening or closing draperies, shades, or skylights.

_____ 10. Playing back a recorded phone message.

_____ 11. Recognizing intruder actions and movements.

_____ 12. Sensing heating and cooling levels.

_____ 13. Setting climate controls to register different temperatures for active and inactive periods.

_____ 14. Signaling appliances to begin operating.

_____ 15. Sounding a siren.

_____ 16. Timing light controls to make the home appear "lived-in" while the family is away on vacation.

_____ 17. Turning an audio or entertainment system on.

_____ 18. Turning lights on or off.

_____ 19. Using a phone to control appliances remotely.

_____ 20. Using an intercom.

Column B

A. alarm functions

B. communication/recording functions

C. monitoring functions

D. programming functions

E. switching functions

Security-System Components

Activity 21-2

Name _____

Date _____

Match each term below with its description by writing the proper term in each box.

control panel   door sensor   glassbreak detector
motion detector   panic button   shock sensor
siren   smoke detector   touch pad

1. [   ]   Provides a method of telling the system what to do.

2. [   ]   Should be located on every level of the home.

3. [   ]   The brains of a security system.

4. [   ]   Provides a warning to intruders.

5. [   ]   Detects an intruder inside the home.

6. [   ]   Works in conjunction with the glassbreak detector.

7. [   ]   Protects against unauthorized entry.

8. [   ]   Sends a silent alarm to a monitoring station.

9. [   ]   Set at the frequency of breaking glass.

Home Automation
Activity 21-3

Name _____

Date _____

Select a floor plan in the textbook or one provided by your instructor and plan the location of each component for a home security and automation system. Draw the plan manually or with the appropriate computer program, using a ¼ in. = 1 ft. scale. Use the proper symbols. (Refer to "A-4, Electrical Symbols" in the text's appendix.) Record your instructor's directions in the space below. Attach your finished work to this page.

Important notes:_____

_____

_____

_____

_____

_____

_____

_____

_____

_____

_____

_____

_____

_____

_____

_____

_____

_____

_____

_____

_____

_____

_____

_____

_____

_____

_____

Chapter 22
Energy and Water Conservation

Check Your Understanding

Name _____

Date _____

Short Answer: Provide brief responses to the following questions or statements.

1. Why is it important for houses to be insulated? _____

    _____

    _____

2. What type of insulation is best for a 100-year-old house being restored? The original siding will be scraped and repainted, and the plaster on the interior walls will be wallpapered. _____

    _____

3. Why is air circulation important in attics? _____

    _____

    _____

4. Name two technological improvements that have made furnaces more efficient. _____

    _____

    _____

5. Select two service-area appliances and discuss their energy-conserving features. _____

    _____

    _____

    _____

    _____

    _____

    _____

    _____

    _____

    _____

    _____

(continued)

Name_____

Date _____

6. What drawbacks or problems are related to using solar energy as a heat source for homes?

_____

_____

_____

_____

_____

_____

_____

_____

_____

7. How can computers play a part in managing a home's energy use? _____

_____

_____

_____

_____

_____

_____

_____

_____

_____

_____

Multiple Choice: Select the best response and write the letter in the preceding blank.

_____ 8. The type of insulation with the highest R-value per unit of thickness is _____.
   A. a blanket
   B. a board
   C. loose fill
   D. fiberglass

_____ 9. Loose-fill insulation is made from _____.
   A. mineral fiber
   B. cellulose fiber
   C. expanded materials such as perlite or vermiculite
   D. All of the above.

_____ 10. Generally, the location of the greatest amount of heat loss is _____.
   A. around windows
   B. between the foundation and the side wall
   C. between the ceiling and roof
   D. None of the above.

(continued)

Name _____

Date _____

_____ 11. To take advantage of prevailing breezes in warm weather, windows should be placed _____.
　　　　　　　A. near exterior corners and high on walls
　　　　　　　B. near exterior corners and midway between ceilings and floors
　　　　　　　C. away from exterior corners and midway between ceilings and floors
　　　　　　　D. away from exterior corners and high on walls

_____ 12. Homes in warm climates should have _____ colored roofs to reflect heat.
　　　　　　　A. dark
　　　　　　　B. light
　　　　　　　C. Both of the above.
　　　　　　　D. None of the above.

_____ 13. Insulation may be extended to the outside of the exterior wall without interfering with attic ventilation when the _____.
　　　　　　　A. soffit is level with the ceiling
　　　　　　　B. soffit is higher than the ceiling
　　　　　　　C. soffit is lower than the ceiling
　　　　　　　D. None of the above.

_____ 14. An EnergyGuide label _____.
　　　　　　　A. is required on all appliances
　　　　　　　B. shows the actual operating cost of the appliance for a year
　　　　　　　C. estimates the annual operating cost of the appliance
　　　　　　　D. None of the above.

_____ 15. For small tasks requiring hot water such as shaving, the ideal appliance to install under bathroom and kitchen sinks is a _____.
　　　　　　　A. heat pump
　　　　　　　B. small, on-demand water heater
　　　　　　　C. hot water-bank recovery unit
　　　　　　　D. None of the above.

_____ 16. A factor preventing greater use of windmills as an alternative energy source by homeowners is _____.
　　　　　　　A. cost
　　　　　　　B. objections from public utility companies
　　　　　　　C. Public Utilities Regulatory Policy Act of 1978
　　　　　　　D. insufficient wind

Completion: Complete the following sentences by writing the missing words in the preceding blanks.

_____ 17. About _____ percent of a home's air infiltration occurs around exterior window frames.

_____ 18. A wide overhang shades the south side of a house from the summer sun, which has a _____ angle in summer than in winter.

_____ 19. Exterior walls may be _____ framed to permit more space for insulation.

_____ 20. Heat pumps are efficient sources of home heating until the outside temperature drops to approximately _____ °F.

_____ 21. Household toilets use no more than _____ gallons of water per flush.

_____ 22. _____ buildings use materials that are considered environmentally friendly.

Orientation
Activity 22-1

Name _____

Date _____

Study Figures 22-1 and 22-2 in your text, which show recommended orientations for various rooms of a house in cold and warm climates. Specify the compass orientation of each room in the two climates. Then explain why different solar orientations are needed for the two climates.

	Cold Climate	**Warm Climate**
1. Living room	_____	_____
2. Dining room	_____	_____
3. Kitchen	_____	_____
4. Porch	_____	_____
5. Bedrooms	_____	_____
6. Master bedroom	_____	_____
7. Utility	_____	_____
8. Garage	_____	_____

9. Explanation: _____

_____

_____

_____

_____

_____

_____

_____

_____

_____

_____

_____

_____

_____

_____

_____

Insulation
Activity 22-2

Name _____

Date _____

Match the descriptions in Column A with the correct insulation terms in Column B. Place the appropriate letter in each blank.

Column A

_____   1. Includes perlite and vermiculite.

_____   2. Is thick and flexible, and may be cut or curved to fit the space to be insulated.

_____   3. Has a 4.00 R-value per inch.

_____   4. Made of rigid, foamed plastics.

_____   5. Is available in blanket, board, and loose-fill forms.

_____   6. Is often used in inaccessible spaces.

_____   7. Has a 0.11 R-value per inch.

_____   8. Should be placed between the interior of the room and the insulation.

_____   9. Is insulation without a vapor barrier.

_____ 10. Has a 0.91 R-value per inch.

Column B

A. blanket insulation

B. expanded material

C. face brick

D. hardwoods

E. insulation

F. insulation boards

G. loose-fill insulation

H. unfaced insulation

I. vapor barrier

J. wood fiber insulation

Increasing Efficiency
Activity 22-3

Name _____

Date _____

Write an essay about the ways to increase the heating and cooling efficiency of a dwelling. Include facts presented in the text and other sources. Your discussion should include architectural considerations such as: orientation of the home; insulation, placement, and construction of windows and doors; construction of roofs and walls; placement of heating and plumbing systems; and landscaping techniques that can help conserve energy.

_____

_____

_____

_____

_____

_____

_____

_____

_____

_____

_____

_____

_____

_____

_____

_____

_____

_____

_____

_____

_____

_____

_____

_____

_____

_____

Chapter 23
Designing for Health and Safety

Check Your Understanding

Name _____

Date _____

Multiple Choice: Select the best response and write the letter in the preceding blanks.

_____ 1. Class C fire extinguishers are used on fires involving _____.
A. paper
B. fabric
C. burning liquids
D. electrical devices

_____ 2. A _____ is *not* generally a source of water vapor in the house.
A. roof leak
B. wet plaster
C. wet basement
D. drippy hose bib

_____ 3. Fire safety code requirements mandate that all stairs must be at least _____ ft. wide.
A. 28
B. 32
C. 36
D. 40

_____ 4. A tropical storm is classified as a hurricane when winds reach a constant speed of _____ mph or more.
A. 64
B. 74
C. 84
D. 94

_____ 5. The area along the Mississippi River called the _____ region is an earthquake zone.
A. Louisiana Delta
B. Mississippi Valley
C. New Madrid
D. Missouri Basin

_____ 6. Long-term radon testing devices require more than _____ days.
A. 30
B. 50
C. 70
D. 90

_____ 7. Tornadoes are most frequent in the United States during _____.
A. January through March
B. April through June.
C. July through September
D. October through December

(continued)

Name _____

Date _____

_____ 8. The natural hazard responsible for more property damage and deaths in the country than any destructive force of nature is _____.
   A. fires
   B. tornadoes
   C. hurricanes
   D. flooding

_____ 9. The number of U.S. fire deaths that occur in the home is _____ percent.
   A. 60
   B. 70
   C. 80
   D. 90

_____ 10. The states having the greatest number of tornadoes are _____.
   A. Florida, Georgia, and Alabama
   B. Missouri, Ohio, and Illinois
   C. Texas, Oklahoma, and Kansas
   D. Nebraska, North Dakota, and Minnesota

Completion: Complete the following sentences by writing the missing words in the preceding blanks.

_____ 11. Class B fire extinguishers are used for _____ fires.

_____ 12. Carbon monoxide poisoning reduces the blood's ability to transport _____.

_____ 13. Radon comes from the natural decay of _____ found in soil, rock, and water.

_____ 14. Reducing radon is called radon _____.

_____ 15. *Stachybotrys atra* is a greenish-black _____.

_____ 16. About one-third of the accidental deaths occurring in U.S. homes each year are due to _____.

_____ 17. Molds break down plant materials by _____.

Short Answer: Provide brief answers to the following questions or statements.

18. Name two of the leading causes of residential fires. _____

   _____

   _____

   _____

19. What causes a smoke detector to chirp? _____

   _____

20. What is the minimum allowable width of an exit path from a bedroom? _____

   _____

21. For what type of materials is the Class A fire extinguisher designed?_____

   _____

(continued)

Name _____

Date _____

22. What is carbon monoxide (CO)? _____

_____

23. What are the symptoms of low-level carbon monoxide poisoning? _____

_____

_____

_____

24. How does radon enter a home? _____

_____

_____

_____

25. When should a home be tested for radon? _____

_____

26. What is the most common visual example of condensation in the home? _____

_____

27. What are some of the most common sources of water vapor inside the home?_____

_____

_____

_____

28. What is the purpose of foundation vents? _____

_____

29. How do molds reproduce? _____

_____

30. What types of health problems generally result from exposure to molds? _____

_____

_____

_____

31. What should be done to reduce the risk of fire from gas appliances during an earthquake?

_____

_____

(continued)

Name_____

Date _____

32. What is a flash flood? _____

_____

_____

33. What does the term *100-year floodplain* mean? _____

_____

34. What time of day do most tornadoes form? _____

_____

35. When is the U.S. hurricane season? _____

_____

36. What is the purpose of hurricane codes? _____

_____

37. What are the four major causes of accidents in the home?_____

_____

_____

_____

Fire, Gas, and Mold
Activity 23-1

Name _____

Date _____

Match the descriptions in Column A with the correct terms in Column B. Place the appropriate letter in each blank. (Letters are used more than once.)

Column A

_____ 1. Associated with combustion appliances.

_____ 2. Can be caused by burning green wood.

_____ 3. Can be removed with a household bleach and water mixture.

_____ 4. Can be stopped with the appropriate Class A, B, or C extinguisher.

_____ 5. Can cause brain damage, heart attacks, or death at high levels.

_____ 6. Causes respiratory difficulties, sore throat, and skin and eye irritation at low levels, but can even cause death.

_____ 7. Enters through cracks in the walls and floors.

_____ 8. Inhibits the blood's ability to transport oxygen.

_____ 9. Is a radioactive gas.

_____ 10. Is responsible for the formation of spores.

_____ 11. Is the second-leading cause of lung cancer.

_____ 12. Linked to moisture problems in the home.

_____ 13. Poses the greatest danger during heating and air-conditioning periods.

_____ 14. Produces smoke.

_____ 15. Produces symptoms similar to the flu at low levels.

_____ 16. Results from the incomplete burning of fuel.

Column B

A. carbon monoxide

B. fire

C. mold

D. radon

Preventing Property Damage and Injury
Activity 23-2

Name _____

Date _____

Match four types of hazards with the safety practices described below. Place the letter preceding each safety practice in the correct box. (Letters may be used more than once.)

1. Earthquakes _____

2. Tornadoes _____

3. Hurricanes _____

4. Unsafe Interiors _____

Safety Practices

A. Remove items outside the home that might become flying debris.

B. Remove trip-hazards from traffic circulation patterns.

C. Build a safe room.

D. Follow the recommendations of the CCCL.

E. Install a roof covering designed to resist high winds.

F. Secure hanging items to the permanent structure of the home.

G. Remove combustible materials from nearby heaters and fireplaces.

H. Install a garage door that can withstand at least 110 mph winds.

I. Limit the use of extension cords.

J. Use straps or cables to secure large items to the wall.

Chapter 24
Exterior Design

Check Your Understanding

Name _____

Date _____

Matching: Match the descriptions in Column A with the terms in Column B. Place the appropriate letter in each blank.

Column A

_____ 1. Includes scrolls and gingerbread that surround eaves, windows, and doors.

_____ 2. Includes Greek and Roman features.

_____ 3. Named after a container used to store a cooking ingredient in Colonial America.

_____ 4. Has a characteristic band of stone between the first and second floor.

_____ 5. Has a characteristic square tower at the top of the house.

_____ 6. Has an overhanging second story that characterizes the style.

_____ 7. Is often used for government buildings.

_____ 8. Includes a gable roof and central fireplace in a small 1½-story house.

_____ 9. Has a front colonnade and giant two-story portico.

_____ 10. Includes a large central chimney and gambrel roof.

Column B

A. Cape Ann

B. Cape Cod

C. Federal

D. garrison

E. Georgian

F. Greek Revival

G. Italianate

H. saltbox

I. Southern Colonial

J. Victorian

Multiple Choice: Select the best response and write the letter in the preceding blank.

_____ 11. The adobe home has a _____.
A. flat roof
B. mission tile roof
C. low pitch roof
D. gable roof

_____ 12. The log cabin was brought to America by _____ immigrants.
A. German
B. Swedish
C. French
D. English

(continued)

202 Chapter 24 Exterior Design

Name _____

Date _____

_____ 13. Pennsylvania Dutch Colonial homes are made of thick, fieldstone walls because the material _____.
    A. was used in their native Germany
    B. provided the support needed for the heavy roof
    C. kept the house warm and was easy to maintain
    D. None of the above.

_____ 14. A feature of the French plantation house is a _____.
    A. gambrel roof that flares out at the bottom and extends to cover a porch
    B. small roof ledge between the first and second floor, called a pent roof
    C. turret that was used to store grain
    D. hip roof that extends into a very broad roof and covers a porch surrounding the house

_____ 15. An important characteristic of the French manor is the _____ roof on the manor and dovecote roofs on the wings.
    A. gable
    B. gambrel
    C. Mansard
    D. hip

_____ 16. Compact size and a very steep gable roof are predominant features of the _____ that originated in England.
    A. Tudor manor
    B. Cotswold cottage
    C. Elizabethan manor
    D. half-house

_____ 17. One common feature of a ranch style is the _____.
    A. one-story design
    B. gingerbread
    C. tall, thin windows
    D. wrought iron trim

_____ 18. Buckminster Fuller's geodesic dome is based on the _____.
    A. rectangle
    B. triangle
    C. square
    D. All of the above.

Short Answer: Provide brief answers to the following questions or statements.

19. Describe three features of a Spanish style house. _____

_____

_____

_____

20. What is the most distinguishing feature of the Dutch Colonial style house? _____

_____

_____

(continued)

Name _____

Date _____

21. Some French Normandy houses use half-timber walls for decoration. Explain what these are.

_____

_____

22. Describe the features of a Louisiana French style house. _____

_____

_____

23. List two features that are found in both the Tudor style and Elizabethan style manor. _____

_____

_____

24. Identify two advantages of split-level style homes._____

_____

_____

25. What was Frank Lloyd Wright's main goal when designing a home? _____

_____

26. What features inside a solar home can collect and store heat? _____

_____

_____

_____

27. On which side of the house are solar features most functional? _____

_____

28. Briefly describe a site that would be ideal for an earth-sheltered home._____

_____

Architectural Style Identification

Activity 24-1

Name _____

Date _____

Take a photograph, clip a picture from a magazine, or sketch an example of a residence that clearly illustrates a basic architectural style and mount the illustration in the space provided. Then identify the style and list its key characteristics.

Mount illustration here.

The architectural style is: _____

The key characteristics are: _____

_____

_____

_____

_____

_____

_____

_____

_____

House Styles
Activity 24-2

Name _____

Date _____

Using the following terms, identify each of the basic architectural home styles shown below.

Cape Ann
Dutch Colonial
Federal

Pennsylvania Dutch
Saltbox
Southern Colonial

Spanish
Tudor

1. _____

2. _____

3. _____

4. _____

5. _____

6. _____

7. _____

8. _____

Contemporary Homes
Activity 24-3

Name _____

Date _____

Select one of the contemporary designs discussed in the text (geodesic domes, foam domes, solar homes, or underground structures) and write an essay describing how living in it might appeal to you. Describe how your lifestyle, feelings, and attitudes might be affected by the unique structure.

_____

_____

_____

_____

_____

_____

_____

_____

_____

_____

_____

_____

_____

_____

_____

_____

_____

_____

_____

_____

_____

_____

_____

_____

_____

_____

_____

_____

_____

Chapter 25
Landscaping

Check Your Understanding

Name _____

Date _____

Multiple Choice: Select the best response and write the letter in the preceding blank.

_____ 1. The most important factor in choosing a lawn grass is _____.
A. cost
B. the setting
C. its tolerance for a given climate
D. None of the above.

_____ 2. Trees that have blossoms or leaves with interesting shapes or colors are _____.
A. native deciduous
B. ornamental
C. narrow-leafed evergreen
D. broad-leaved evergreen

_____ 3. Of the following choices, the tree most suitable for use in a grouping near the corner of a house is _____.
A. incense cedar
B. crab apple
C. star magnolia
D. hickory

_____ 4. A tree native to most of the country is _____.
A. mountain ash
B. Carolina hemlock
C. American holly
D. honey locust

_____ 5. A shrub with beautiful yellow blossoms in early spring is _____.
A. smoke bush
B. forsythia
C. dwarf burning bush
D. privet

_____ 6. A shrub that functions as a narrow-leafed evergreen suited as a foundation plant around a house is _____.
A. sourwood
B. Italian cypress
C. Japanese garden juniper
D. viburnum

_____ 7. Walks tend to be _____ than paths.
A. more formal
B. less formal
C. less permanent
D. less expensive

(continued)

Name _____

Date _____

_____ 8. An informal, less permanent structure that can be used to define a boundary is a _____.
A. fence
B. wall
C. bank
D. All of the above.

_____ 9. The _____ zone is the ideal space for lawn games.
A. public
B. private
C. service
D. recreation

_____ 10. A landscape will be more interesting with _____.
A. shrubs of different varieties
B. ornamental trees
C. a variety of trees, shrubs, grasses, and ground covers
D. landscape elements of the same height

_____ 11. The plants that most convey a feeling of height are the _____.
A. ornamental trees
B. deciduous shrubs
C. broad conical evergreen trees
D. narrow conical evergreen trees

Short Answer: Provide brief responses to the following questions or statements.

12. Identify five functions that plants provide in the landscape. _____

_____

_____

_____

_____

_____

13. When are ground covers frequently used? _____

_____

14. Contrast the difference between narrow-leafed and broad-leaved evergreen trees. _____

_____

_____

_____

_____

_____

(continued)

Name _____

Date _____

15. Identify the shape of the traditional Christmas tree? _____

_____

16. How are shrubs commonly used in a landscape? _____

_____

_____

17. How are both narrow-leafed and broad-leaved evergreen shrubs used in a landscape?

_____

_____

_____

_____

_____

18. What materials are generally used for paths? _____

_____

_____

19. What factors should be considered when planning a garden wall? _____

_____

_____

_____

20. How do decks and patios differ? _____

_____

_____

_____

21. Identify the steps used in planning the landscape. _____

_____

_____

_____

_____

_____

(continued)

Name _____

Date _____

22. List the main zones of a residential landscape. _____

_____

23. How are lines used in a landscape?_____

_____

_____

_____

_____

24. How can interest be created by using color in a landscape?_____

_____

_____

_____

_____

25. When planning a landscape and considering the proportion of elements, what plant sizes should be kept in mind? _____

_____

_____

26. What type of balance is probably best for the landscape of a French Normandy cottage?_____

_____

Ornamental Plants
Activity 25-1

Name _____

Date _____

Prepare a chart of plants that thrive in your area of the country. Contact your local library, plant nursery, or county extension agent for specific information.

Lawn Grasses

Common Name	Sun Conditions	Propagation

Ground Cover Plants

Common Name	Lighting Requirements	Type and Use

Native Deciduous Trees

Common Name	Height and Spread	Characteristics

Ornamental Trees

Common Name	Height and Spread	Characteristics

(continued)

Name _____

Date _____

Evergreen Trees

Common Name	Basic Shape	Mature Height

Shrubs

Common Name	Height	Characteristics

Other Plants

Common Name	Height and Shape	Characteristics

Landscape Plan
Activity 25-2

Name _____

Date _____

Select plants that thrive in your area of the country for use in the landscape plan below. Assign a plant for each symbol used in the plan and write the name of the plant in the space provided.

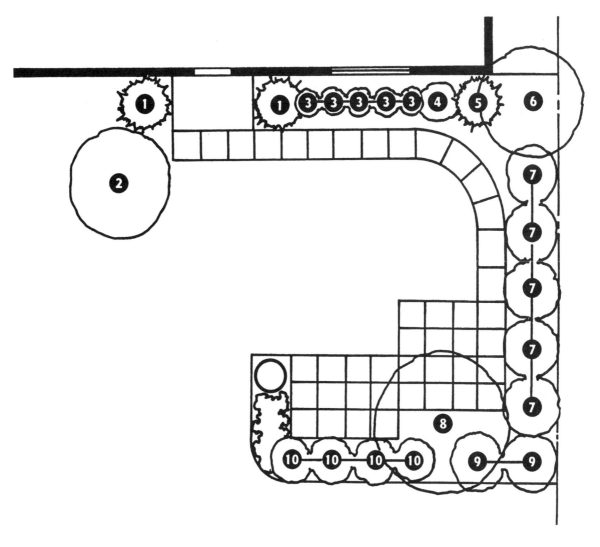

1. _____   6. _____

2. _____   7. _____

3. _____   8. _____

4. _____   9. _____

5. _____   10. _____

Planning a Landscape
Activity 25-3

Name _____

Date _____

Plan a landscape of your own design that follows the suggestions presented on pages 454-458 of your text. Use the chart you developed in Activity 25-1, "Ornamental Plants," to help choose plants appropriate for your area. Select a scale that will show your entire design below.

The scale for this landscape plan is: _____

Chapter 26
Remodeling, Renovation, and Preservation

Check Your Understanding

Name _____

Date _____

Matching: Match the job responsibilities in Column A with the job titles in Column B. Place the appropriate letter in each space. (Letters may be used more than once.)

Column A

_____ 1. Helps to determine if remodeling plans comply to building, plumbing, and electrical codes.

_____ 2. Helps select and coordinate fabric samples and paint chips.

_____ 3. Does the actual remodeling work.

_____ 4. Makes final drawings of the proposed plan.

_____ 5. Makes suggestions to improve the design or function of any material in a room.

_____ 6. Schedules the subcontractors needed.

_____ 7. Writes specifications for materials.

_____ 8. Obtains required building permits.

_____ 9. Helps to maintain the overall exterior design.

_____ 10. May supervise the remodeling work.

_____ 11. Helps evaluate the floor plan.

Column B

A. architect

B. contractor

C. interior designer

Short Answer: Provide brief answers to the following questions or statements below.

12. Identify three reasons why a family might decide to remodel their present home rather than buy a new one. _____

_____

_____

_____

_____

_____

(continued)

Name _____

Date _____

13. Would remodeling be recommended to a growing family that is planning to stay in the current home for five or six more years? Explain. _____

_____

_____

_____

_____

_____

_____

_____

_____

_____

14. Name at least two factors that would persuade a family to remodel unused space rather than build an addition. _____

_____

_____

_____

_____

_____

_____

_____

15. What information should be obtained before making a decision to remodel? _____

_____

_____

_____

_____

_____

16. What are the advantages and disadvantages of homeowners doing their own remodeling?

_____

_____

_____

_____

_____

_____

_____

                                    (continued)

Name _____

Date _____

17. Some lived-in areas of the home are more likely to be remodeled than others. Name two lived-in areas that are frequently remodeled. _____

_____

18. Identify some of the improvements that result from remodeling a kitchen. _____

_____

_____

_____

_____

_____

_____

_____

19. Name three uninhabited spaces that can be made livable. _____

_____

20. What additional construction may be needed to convert a garage or porch into a living area?

_____

_____

_____

_____

21. What are the minimum height requirements, including slope, for an attic living space? _____

_____

_____

_____

22. List the two critical factors to consider when converting an attic to a living space. _____

_____

_____

23. How does the time of the year affect constructing additions to a home? _____

_____

_____

(continued)

Name _____

Date _____

24. What should be considered before removing an exterior wall? What precautions should be taken?

_____

_____

_____

_____

_____

25. When a second-story addition is planned, what three steps must be taken to prepare for the new
construction? _____

_____

_____

_____

_____

_____

26. What parts of a house should be closely inspected before buying to remodel? _____

_____

_____

_____

_____

_____

27. A good remodeling job is carefully planned before any work begins. Identify the steps in the
planning process. _____

_____

_____

_____

_____

Multiple Choice: Select the best response and write the letter in the preceding blank.

_____ 28. Remodeling a basement as a bedroom requires _____.
A. an outside entrance to the basement
B. a second stairway
C. at least one window
D. None of the above.

(continued)

Name _____

Date _____

_____ 29. A _____ is placed in a basement to prevent flooding.
  A. dehumidifier
  B. sump pump
  C. vapor barrier
  D. humidifier

_____ 30. When converting an attic to a living space, the floor joists should be inspected to make sure they are strong enough to support a _____.
  A. nonbearing load
  B. dead load
  C. live load
  D. None of the above.

_____ 31. A _____ requires the most time, expense, and construction to provide additional natural lighting to a remodeled attic.
  A. window well
  B. window
  C. skylight
  D. dormer

_____ 32. When a structure is returned to its original condition, it is _____.
  A. restored
  B. adapted for reuse
  C. remodeled
  D. rebuilt

Remodeling an Attic
Activity 26-1

Name _____

Date _____

Write a short essay explaining what needs to be considered when planning to remodel an attic into a studio work space. Address the following topics in your essay: changes to the existing structure, cost of remodeling, the supporting strength of the floor and ceiling below, access to the attic, ventilation and natural lighting, available headroom, insulation, wiring needs, and heating and cooling.

_____

_____

_____

_____

_____

_____

_____

_____

_____

_____

_____

_____

_____

_____

_____

_____

_____

_____

_____

_____

_____

_____

_____

_____

_____

_____

_____

Planning an Addition
Activity 26-2

Name _____

Date _____

Plan a family room addition to the house below and include plans for any other features that will enhance the overall design. Sketch your solution in the space provided, maintaining a relative scale to the existing floor plan.

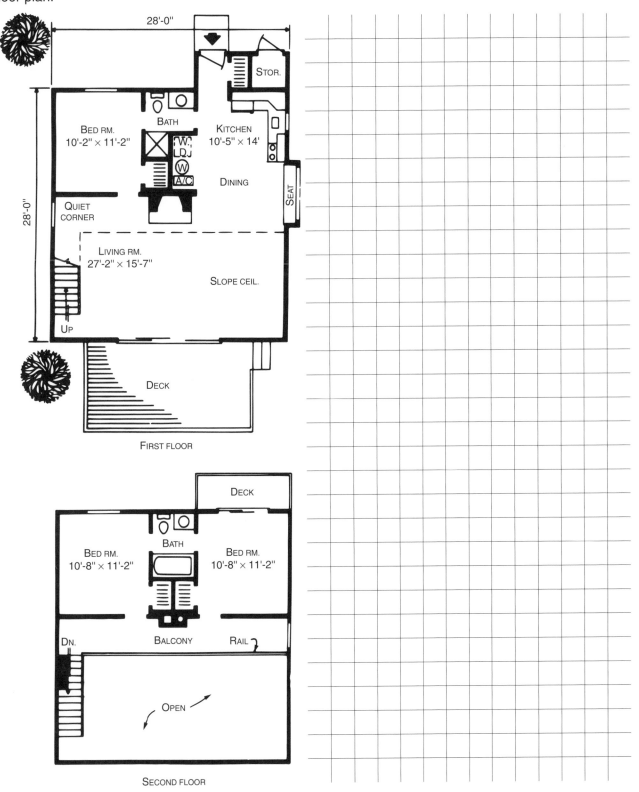

Chapter 27
Presenting Housing Ideas

Check Your Understanding

Name _____

Date _____

Completion: Complete the following sentences by writing the missing words in the preceding blanks.

_____ 1. Exterior perspectives and interior perspectives are two types of _____ drawings.

_____ 2. The _____ perspective is a pictorial of the outside of a structure.

_____ 3. Drawings are given perspective by using _____ points.

_____ 4. Two sides of a building are usually featured in _____-_____ perspectives.

_____ 5. Interior perspectives are usually drawn in _____-_____ perspective.

_____ 6. A presentation _____ is used by some presenters to illustrate how built-in storage will appear.

_____ 7. To help clients better understand the internal layout of a structure, presentation _____ are used.

_____ 8. Adding realism to a line drawing with shades, shadows, texture, and color is _____.

_____ 9. Professional illustrators can achieve a realistic appearance and smooth gradation of tones with _____ rendering.

Short Answer: Provide brief answers to the following questions or statements.

10. Why are presentation techniques commonly used?_____

_____

11. The vanishing point may be changed to show various areas of a structure. Explain why a designer would want to vary the vanishing point on different perspectives. _____

_____

_____

_____

12. What type of drawing is commonly used to show how interior rooms or space will appear?

_____

13. Identify a type of drawing generally used to evaluate room arrangement and traffic circulation.

_____

(continued)

Name _____

Date _____

14. List two reasons for selecting appliqué rendering. _____

_____

_____

15. Why is the presentation board an important tool for the designer? _____

_____

_____

16. How are models useful to the designer? _____

_____

_____

_____

17. How are slides helpful to the designer? _____

_____

_____

_____

_____

Multiple Choice: Select the best response and write the letter in the preceding blank.

_____ 18. A top view drawing of property showing streets, sidewalks, and soil contour is a
              presentation _____.
              A. section
              B. elevation
              C. landscape plan
              D. plot plan

_____ 19. A drawing that shows the placement and different species of trees, shrubs, and flowers is
              a presentation _____.
              A. plot plan
              B. landscape plan
              C. elevation
              D. section

_____ 20. Rough, freehand sketches made in the early stages of the design are often in the form
              of _____ renderings.
              A. colored pencil
              B. watercolor
              C. pencil
              D. ink

(continued)

Name _____

Date _____

_____ 21. Renderings that reproduce well are _____ renderings.
   A. ink
   B. pencil
   C. colored pencil
   D. watercolor

_____ 22. Vivid colors or light washes of colors are characteristic of _____ renderings.
   A. ink
   B. pencil
   C. colored pencil
   D. watercolor

_____ 23. A type of color rendering that can easily be accomplished by beginning students is rendering created with _____.
   A. ink
   B. felt-tip marker
   C. colored pencil
   D. watercolor

_____ 24. Only experienced illustrators are accomplished enough to use _____ to produce colorful, dramatic renderings.
   A. colored pencils
   B. felt-tip markers
   C. crayons
   D. None of the above.

Presentation Drawings
Activity 27-1

Name _____

Date _____

Match the descriptions in Column A with the nine types of presentation drawings in Column B. Place the appropriate letter in each blank.

Column A

_____ 1. Features two sides of the object and has two vanishing points.

_____ 2. Shows three walls, the floor, and the ceiling.

_____ 3. Is sometimes used for very tall buildings.

_____ 4. Shows an entire landscape in one plan.

_____ 5. Is a pictorial of the outside of a house.

_____ 6. Represents one side of an object but shows no depth.

_____ 7. Shows a furniture arrangement or a traffic-flow analysis.

_____ 8. Shows the relationship between the site and the structure.

_____ 9. Shows a cutaway view of the house or a series of rooms.

Column B

A. exterior perspective

B. one-point perspective

C. presentation elevation

D. presentation floor plan

E. presentation landscape plan

F. presentation plot plan

G. presentation section

H. three-point perspective

I. two-point perspective

Rendering
Activity 27-2

Name _____

Date _____

Render each of the architectural features below using different rendering techniques, such as pencil on one and ink on the other.

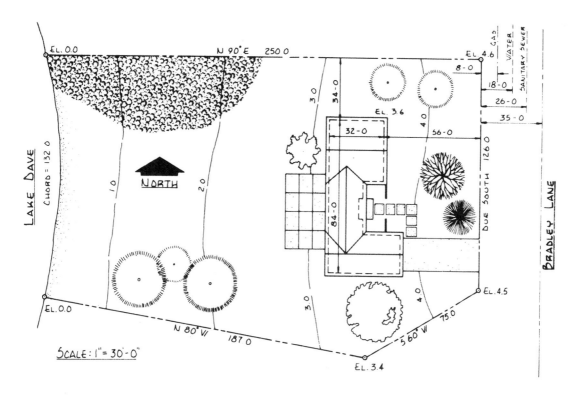

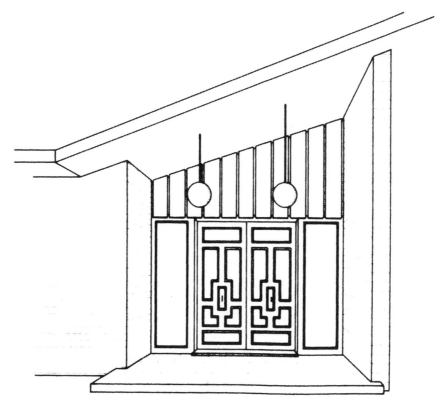

Presentation Board
Activity 27-3

Name _____

Date _____

Prepare a presentation board for a room of your own design. Draw a floor plan of the room and an elevation of each wall at a scale of ¼ *in. = 1 ft.* Use sketches, photos, or magazine pictures to represent furniture chosen for the room. Include fabric, paint, and carpeting samples. Arrange these components on a large piece of mat board or illustration board. Discuss the key points of your presentation in the space below.

Key presentation points: _____

_____

_____

_____

_____

_____

_____

_____

_____

_____

_____

_____

_____

_____

_____

_____

_____

_____

_____

_____

_____

_____

_____

_____

_____

_____

_____

_____

_____

Architectural Model
Activity 27-4

Name _____

Date _____

Build a model of a cabinet, table, chair, or appliance. Use cardboard, foam board, balsa wood, or other suitable material for your project. Select a scale that is appropriate for the project and make each feature as accurate as possible. For example, dollhouse scale is *1 in. = 1 ft.* Sketch your plan below.

The scale is: _____

Chapter 28
Computer Applications

Check Your Understanding

Name _____

Date _____

Short Answer: Provide brief answers to the following questions or statements.

1. List several tasks in the housing field for which computers are used. _____

   _____

   _____

   _____

   _____

   _____

   _____

   _____

   _____

2. Name two advantages of computer-assisted drafting and design (CADD) over traditional manual drafting. _____

   _____

   _____

3. What are three common housing and landscape items that are usually represented in a CADD symbols library? _____

   _____

   _____

4. What features are usually shown in a site plan? _____

   _____

   _____

5. Which two areas of a house are usually the most expensive to build per square foot?

   _____

(continued)

Name _____

Date _____

6. What industry group led the way in developing software programs for kitchen design?

_____

7. Why is computer simulation important to the designer? _____

_____

_____

_____

_____

_____

8. How are software programs supplied by window manufacturers useful to designers? _____

_____

_____

_____

_____

_____

9. What two forces are causing professionals and do-it-yourselfers to turn to application-specific
   software for structural component selection? _____

_____

_____

_____

_____

10. When is a CD-ROM a useful marketing tool? _____

_____

_____

_____

_____

Completion: Complete the following sentences by writing the missing words in the preceding blanks.

_____   11. A plan view drawing that shows the site and locations of buildings on the
                             property is a _____ plan.

_____   12. The computer is very useful in converting _____ data collected by land
                             surveyors into property boundaries, contour lines, and accurate location
                             of features on the site.

(continued)

Name _____

Date _____

_____ 13. Special computer programs for _____ planning programs have an aging feature to show how the appearance of the site will change as the plants mature.

_____ 14. A type of computer program that makes it possible to see the results of a planned structure or system before it is built is computer _____.

_____ 15. Computer programs that communicate information specific to the user's response to questions are called _____.

_____ 16. A _____ chart provides step-by-step guidance in planning and monitoring the construction of a project.

_____ 17. Graphic comparisons of estimated construction schedules versus actual progress performance describes a _____ chart.

Multiple Choice: Select the best response and write the letter in the preceding blank.

_____ 18. The greatest use of computer applications in the housing field is for _____.
   A. determining construction elements and processes
   B. designing and analyzing plans
   C. serving clients
   D. managing projects

_____ 19. In the housing field, a computer is generally not used for _____.
   A. performing cost estimates
   B. presenting designs to clients
   C. retrieving previously designed components
   D. determining a client's taste in furnishings

_____ 20. Of all the benefits that CADD provides, it presents the greatest time savings when _____.
   A. creating drawings
   B. writing the specifications
   C. revising drawings
   D. drawing the actual lines

_____ 21. Generally a landscape plan does not show _____.
   A. typical floor plans
   B. plants on the site
   C. paved areas
   D. fences

_____ 22. An energy analysis is usually performed for a proposed new or remodeled space because it _____.
   A. is a feature clients demand
   B. enables the designer to plan an energy-efficient structure
   C. is required by the profession
   D. is required by law

_____ 23. When selecting kitchen cabinets, software programs prepared by cabinet manufacturers allow computer users to _____.
   A. arrange standard cabinet units into various floor plans
   B. create an order form for the cabinets used in a floor plan
   C. calculate total cost of ordered materials
   D. All of the above.

(continued)

Name _____

Date _____

_____ 24. To improve the scheduling of a construction project, a _____ chart is used.
      A. Gantt
      B. PERT
      C. Both of the above.
      D. Neither of the above.

_____ 25. A computer program for project management in the housing industry will not _____.
      A. improve customer service
      B. result in better cost control
      C. create more accurate CADD drawings
      D. generate quicker response time

Computer Programs
Activity 28-1

Name _____

Date _____

Match the housing tasks described in Column A with computer software applications in Column B. Place the appropriate letter in each blank. (Letters may be used more than once.)

Column A

_____ 1. Analyzing energy reflection and transmission from various surfaces.

_____ 2. Calculating square footage and quantities of materials needed.

_____ 3. Designing and evaluating water-treatment systems.

_____ 4. Evaluating structural members and frames, including cables, beams, and columns.

_____ 5. Examining alternative building materials for increased energy efficiency.

_____ 6. Keeping all project information organized and easily retrievable.

_____ 7. Calculating the volume quantities of earth that must be removed from the site.

_____ 8. Examining the strength and elastic stability of planned building materials.

_____ 9. Inserting standard architectural symbols and shapes automatically into plan drawings.

_____ 10. Mapping land contours.

_____ 11. Keeping track of expenses and payment schedules.

_____ 12. Monitoring progress on a construction project.

_____ 13. Retrieving floor plans and instantly tailoring them to meet specific customer needs.

_____ 14. Evaluating the thermal aspects of solar energy systems.

_____ 15. Reviewing the profit/loss situation.

_____ 16. Studying conditions that will exert force and stress on a structure.

Column B

A. design programs

B. energy analysis programs

C. plot, site, and landscape planning programs

D. project data management programs

E. structural analysis programs

Application-Specific Software
Activity 28-2

Name _____

Date _____

Imagine an area in your home that would benefit from some type of structural change. In a short essay, briefly describe the condition/situation that exists now and the changes you propose. Then identify the computer software application(s) described in your text that could be used on your project. Explain when and how they would be used.

_____

_____

_____

_____

_____

_____

_____

_____

_____

_____

_____

_____

_____

_____

_____

_____

_____

_____

_____

_____

_____

_____

_____

_____

_____

_____

_____

_____

Chapter 29
Careers in Housing

Check Your Understanding

Name _____

Date _____

Matching: Match the job descriptions in Column A with the terms in Column B. Place the appropriate letter in each blank.

Column A

_____ 1. Plans the arrangement and composition of landscape elements on a site.

_____ 2. Works with clients in making sketches, suggesting materials, and helping select the final design plan.

_____ 3. Interviews prospective tenants, maintains property, and reports to the building owner.

_____ 4. Plans and coordinates the construction of buildings.

_____ 5. Assists people in appraising, buying, selling, renting, and leasing property.

_____ 6. Draws the details of working drawings.

_____ 7. Builds scale models of planned communities, buildings, pieces of furniture, or room layouts.

_____ 8. Prepares presentation drawings, sketches, and illustrations.

_____ 9. Includes building inspectors and health inspectors.

_____ 10. Often specializes in estimating and bidding, quality control, or site supervision.

_____ 11. Locates property boundaries, measures distances, establishes contours, and makes drawings of the site surveyed.

_____ 12. Plans and supervises the design and decoration of building interiors.

_____ 13. Operates cranes, bulldozers, backhoes, and forklifts.

_____ 14. Includes carpenters, masons, electricians, plumbers, painters, and paperhangers.

Column B

A. architect

B. architectural drafter

C. architectural illustrator

D. building contractor

E. construction machinery operator

F. construction technologist

G. government positions

H. interior designer

I. land surveyor

J. landscape designer

K. model maker

L. real estate broker

M. real estate manager

N. skilled tradespeople

(continued)

Name _____

Date _____

Short Answer: Provide a brief answer to the following questions or statements.

15. How do the educational requirements of an architect differ from that of an architectural drafter?

_____

_____

_____

_____

_____

_____

16. What special talents and/or experience is necessary to become an architectural illustrator?

_____

_____

17. Identify three tasks an interior designer performs. _____

_____

_____

_____

18. What special knowledge should a landscape designer possess? _____

_____

19. Which tasks does a building contractor perform? _____

_____

_____

20. List the three job levels recognized by most trades. _____

_____

_____

21. What must a person do before he or she can become a registered land surveyor? _____

_____

_____

22. How does training differ for a real estate position as a broker versus a manager? _____

_____

_____

_____

_____

(continued)

Name _____

Date _____

23. Name three valuable U.S. Department of Labor resources that can help you determine a suitable job. _____

_____

_____

_____

_____

24. List five sources to explore for information about job openings. _____

_____

_____

_____

_____

_____

Local Housing Careers
Activity 29-1

Name _____

Date _____

Select a housing career discussed in the text that appeals to you as a career choice. Examine existing local opportunities and interview a practitioner in the field to gain additional insight, if possible. Summarize your findings below.

_____

_____

_____

_____

_____

_____

_____

_____

_____

_____

_____

_____

_____

_____

_____

_____

_____

_____

_____

_____

_____

_____

_____

_____

_____

_____

_____

Exploring Careers
Activity 29-2

Name _____

Date _____

Explore a housing career described in the text by examining the *Occupational Outlook Handbook, Guide for Occupational Exploration,* and O*NET. Write the name of the career on the top line and record the relevant information you find.

	Obtaining a Career as: _____
Academic preparation required	
Experience required	
Training/skills needed	
Personal traits recommended	
Job duties and responsibilities	
Normal work setting	
Beginning and average salary	
Advancement opportunities	
Job outlook	

Chapter 30
Keeping a Job and Advancing a Career

Check Your Understanding

Name _____

Date _____

Multiple Choice: Select the best response and write the letter in the preceding blanks.

_____ 1. Job performance can be measured with _____.
A. general work habits
B. safety record on the job
C. keeping current in the field
D. All of the above are true.

_____ 2. A work habit that is *not* desirable is _____.
A. arguing with your supervisor about your assignment
B. observing safety rules
C. keeping your work area clean and organized
D. observing company policies

_____ 3. Empathic listening is _____.
A. listening with the intent to understand
B. not listening at all
C. pretending to listen
D. selective listening

_____ 4. The item suitable for complete evaluation of form, design, and performance of a housing design plan for a client is _____.
A. computer simulation
B. a prototype
C. a model
D. presentation drawing

_____ 5. An example of an undesirable work ethic is _____.
A. exhibiting enthusiasm for the work
B. working late willingly to meet deadlines
C. having a ready excuse for poor work
D. reporting to work on time

_____ 6. A manager is one who _____.
A. makes and implements decisions
B. accomplishes desired results through others
C. is a leader
D. All of the above.

_____ 7. Negotiation with impartial assistance from someone unaffected by the outcome of the dispute is called _____.
A. resolution
B. mediation
C. negotiation
D. None of the above.

(continued)

Name _____

Date _____

Completion: Complete the following sentences by writing the missing words in the preceding blanks.

_____ 8. Statistics show that only five percent of all accidents are caused by
                            unsafe conditions, while the remainder is caused by unsafe _____.

_____ 9. A _____ model is used to show the construction of a product.

_____ 10. "Rules or standards governing the conduct of the members of a
                            profession" defines _____.

_____ 11. The belief or guiding philosophy that motivates a person to do a good job
                            is called a _____ ethic.

_____ 12. The ability to know what needs to be done now and in the future is called
                            _____.

_____ 13. To assign authority or responsibility to another is to _____.

_____ 14. Hostility resulting from opposing views is _____.

_____ 15. A person who starts, manages, and assumes the risks of a new business
                            is a(n) _____.

Short Answer: Provide brief responses to the following questions or statements.

16. What is the first step in meeting a client's needs? _____

_____

17. Name the four basic types of communication. _____

_____

18. List five primary qualities of successful leaders. _____

_____

_____

_____

_____

_____

19. Identify five characteristics of successful entrepreneurs. _____

_____

_____

_____

_____

_____

_____

20. Name two actions that could be taken to better manage home and work responsibilities. _____

_____

_____

_____

Working with Clients
Activity 30-1

Name _____

Date _____

Imagine you work for a firm that designs homes and home additions and also provides interior design services. Consider the following issues that arise while meeting a new client for the first time. Record what you would say and do at each point.

1. The client wants to expand her kitchen to provide more counterspace and possibly add a mudroom with a half-bath near the service entrance. (Describe your response.) _____

   _____

   _____

   _____

   _____

   _____

   _____

   _____

2. The client has a hard time describing her design preferences. She keeps calling them "mixed." (Describe your response.) _____

   _____

   _____

   _____

   _____

   _____

   _____

   _____

3. The client insists on a timetable that you know is impossible. (Describe your response.)_____

   _____

   _____

   _____

   _____

   _____

   _____

   _____

(continued)

Name _____

Date _____

4. The client emphasizes that she does not want any of the remodeling work to disrupt her family's activities. (Describe your response.)_____

_____

_____

_____

_____

_____

_____

5. You learn during the interview that the client's husband likes the current kitchen and has a negative view of his wife's remodeling plans. (Describe your response.) _____

_____

_____

_____

_____

_____

_____

6. The client has no experience in working with a design firm and wonders if your fees are high compared to those of your competitors. (Describe your response.)_____

_____

_____

_____

_____

_____

_____

Model Ethics Code
Activity 30-2

Name _____

Date _____

Select a career in the housing industry and list 10 points that you would include in its ethics code.

Ethics Code for a career as: _____

1. To _____

_____

_____

2. To _____

_____

_____

3. To _____

_____

_____

4. To _____

_____

_____

5. To _____

_____

_____

6. To _____

_____

_____

7. To _____

_____

_____

8. To _____

_____

_____

9. To _____

_____

_____

10. To _____

_____

_____

Furniture Templates

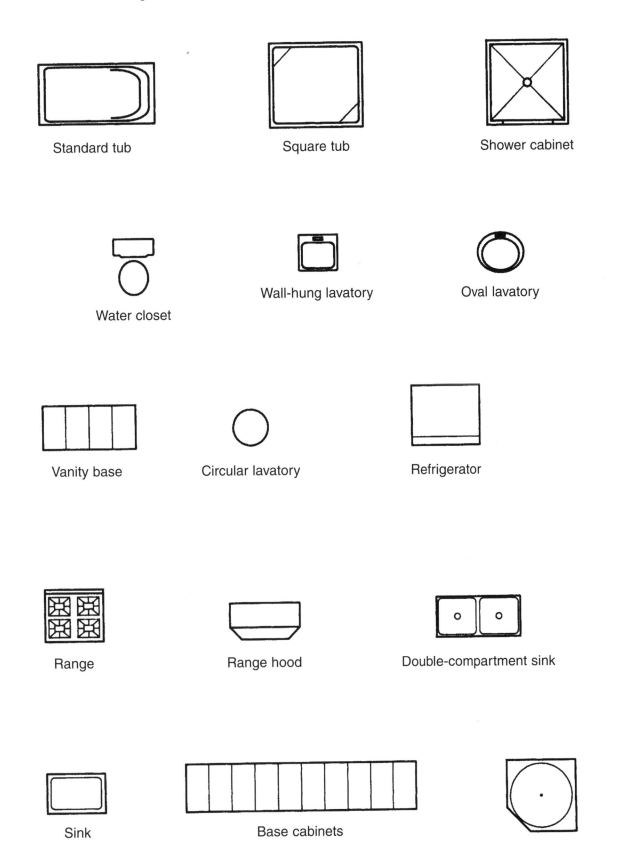

Standard tub

Square tub

Shower cabinet

Water closet

Wall-hung lavatory

Oval lavatory

Vanity base

Circular lavatory

Refrigerator

Range

Range hood

Double-compartment sink

Sink

Base cabinets

Corner cabinet

SCALE: ¼" = 1'-0"

Furniture Templates

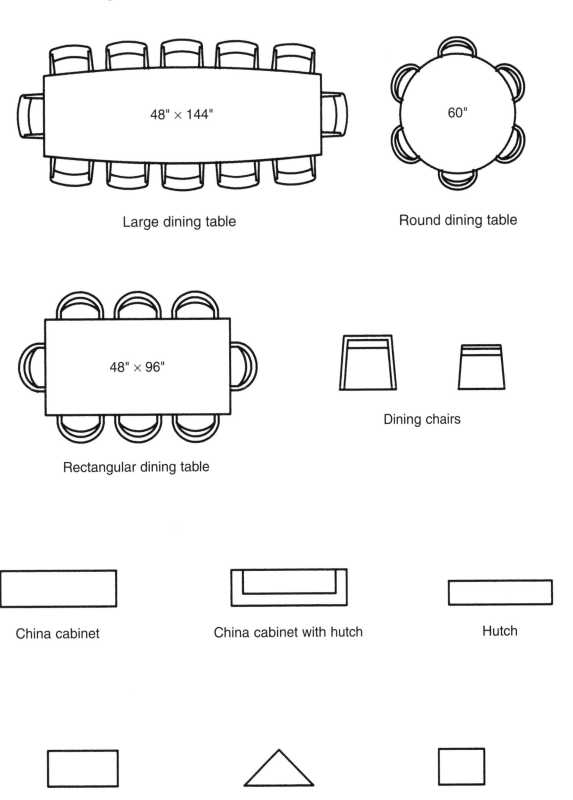

Large dining table

Round dining table

Rectangular dining table

Dining chairs

China cabinet

China cabinet with hutch

Hutch

Server or cart

Corner cabinet

Silver chest

SCALE: ¼" = 1'-0"

Furniture Templates

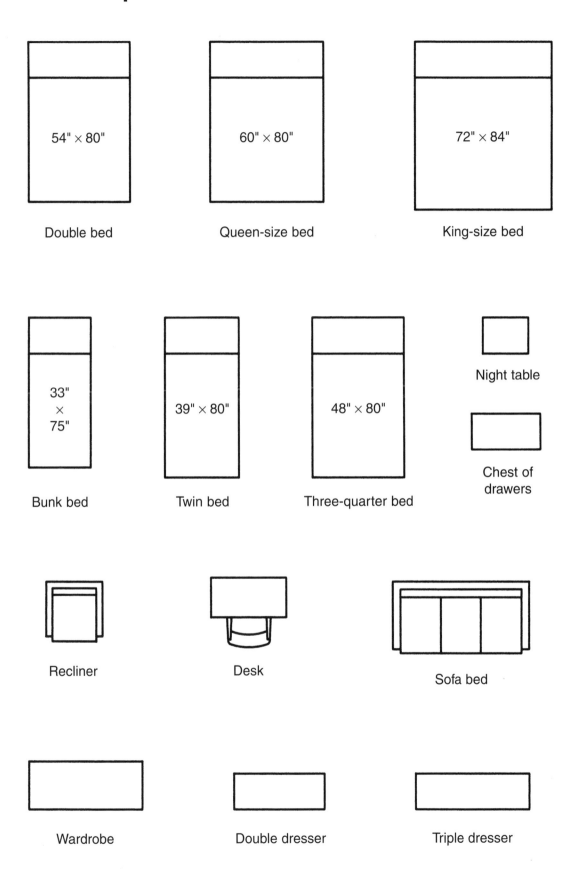

54" × 80"

Double bed

60" × 80"

Queen-size bed

72" × 84"

King-size bed

33"
×
75"

Bunk bed

39" × 80"

Twin bed

48" × 80"

Three-quarter bed

Night table

Chest of
drawers

Recliner

Desk

Sofa bed

Wardrobe

Double dresser

Triple dresser

SCALE: ¼" = 1'-0"

Furniture Templates

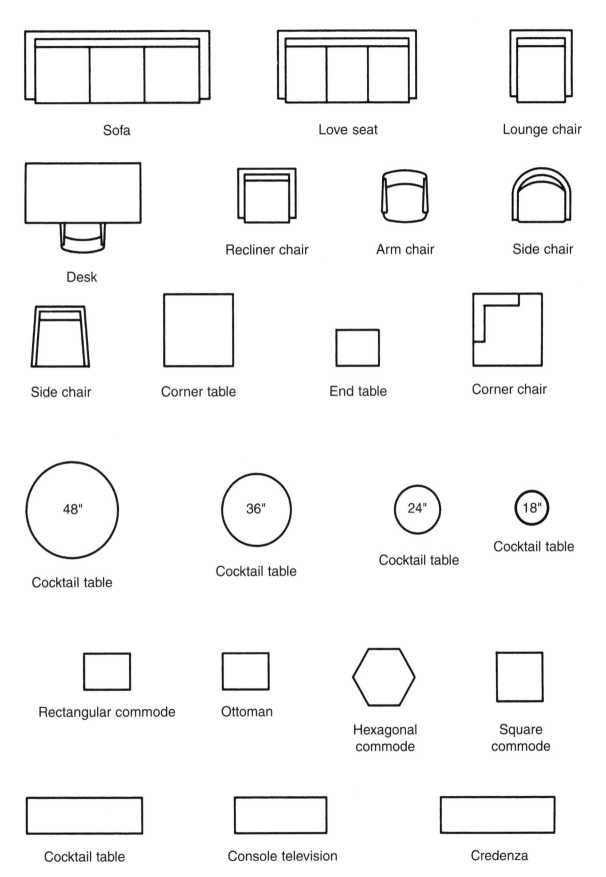

Sofa

Love seat

Lounge chair

Desk

Recliner chair

Arm chair

Side chair

Side chair

Corner table

End table

Corner chair

48"

Cocktail table

36"

Cocktail table

24"

Cocktail table

18"

Cocktail table

Rectangular commode

Ottoman

Hexagonal
commode

Square
commode

Cocktail table

Console television

Credenza

SCALE: ¼" = 1'-0"

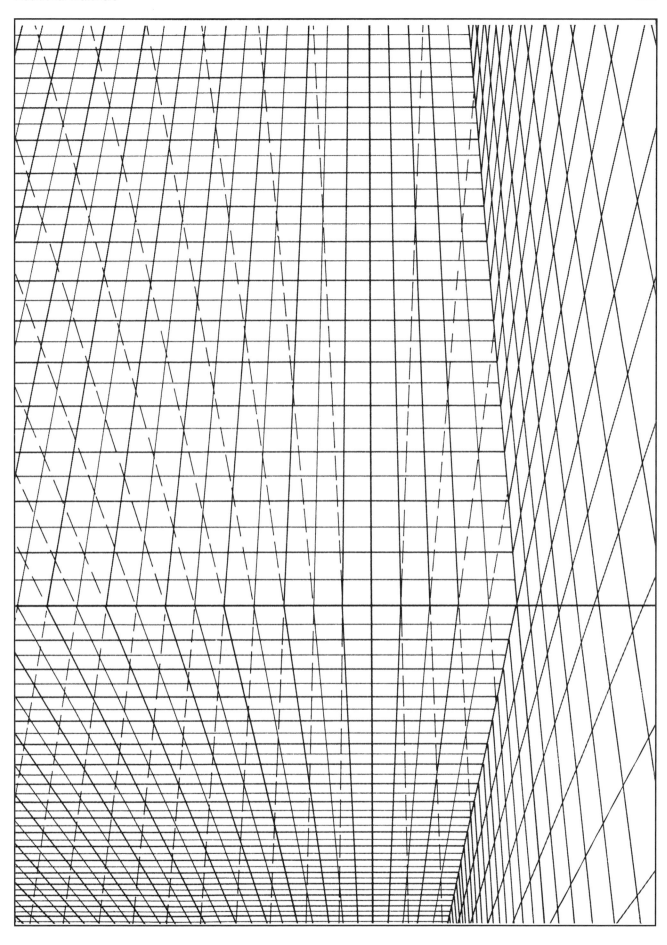

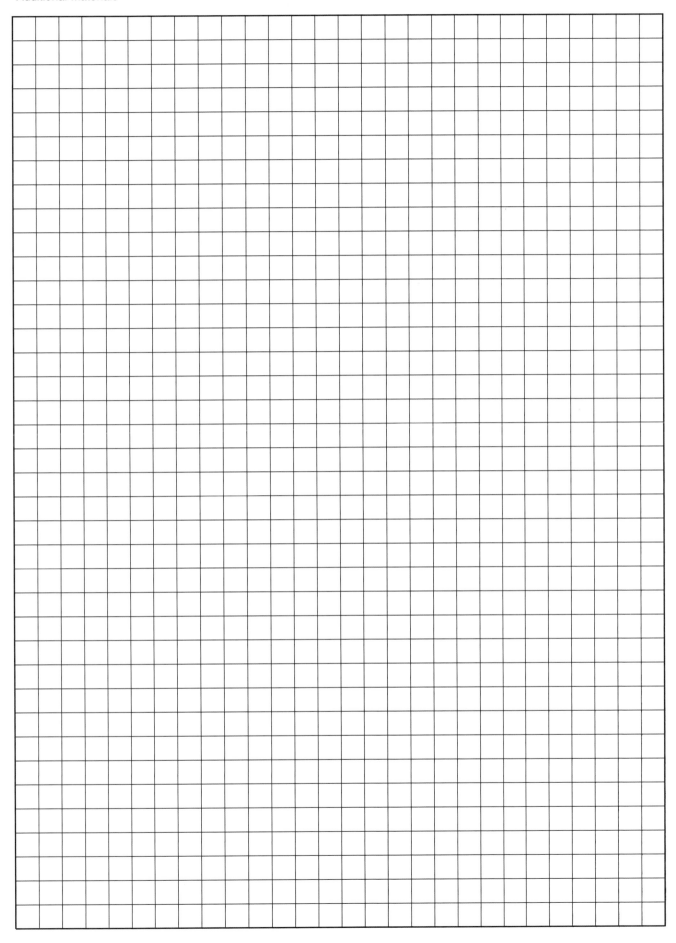